Braving the Storm

By the same author:

Trust: Enduring Hope, a Spring Harvest workbook published by Authentic, 2006.

Braving the Storm

Survival Tactics

Eric Gaudion

Authentic

LONDON ● ATLANTA ● HYDERABAD

13 12 11 10 09 08 07   7 6 5 4 3 2 1

First published 2007 by Authentic Media
9 Holdom Avenue, Bletchley, Milton Keynes, MK1 1QR, UK
285 Lynnwood Avenue, Tyrone, GA 30290, USA
OM Authentic Media, Medchal Road, Jeedimetla Village,
Secunderabad 500 055, A.P., India

www.authenticmedia.co.uk
Authentic Media is a division of Send the Light Ltd., a company limited
by guarantee (registered charity no. 270162)

British Library Cataloguing in Publication Data
A catalogue record for this book is available from the British Library

ISBN-13: 978-1-85078-739-6
ISBN-10: 1-85078-739-5

Cover Design by fourninezero design.
Typeset by GCS
Print Management by Adare Carwin
Printed and Bound in Great Britain by J.H. Haynes & Co., Sparkford

Contents

Acknowledgements

I would like to thank Jeff Lucas, Alison Hull and
Sheila Jacobs for their encouragement and help
in getting this book published.

I also want to thank the wonderful folk at Shiloh
Church, Guernsey for their amazing patience with
me through all my struggles and pain. Thanks, too,
to Sandie Ward, Dr Peter Richards, and Dr Stephen
Pereira without whom I may not have been here to
tell the tale!

Most of all, my thanks to Diane, my partner
in pain and to Matthew who has been there
for me all the way.

Foreword

'Though there's pain in the offering, blessed be your name'.[1]

The poignant line from Matt Redman's powerful song is so very easy to sing – and so very difficult to live. To bless the God of the heavens is easy when the sun is shining in a clear blue sky. But when you find yourself caught in what seems to be a never-ending downpour, when you are forced to turn your collar up and put your head down against the wind – now that's another story. On the worst days, often many clouds gather at once. The author of this book has been battling with years of excruciating physical agony, exhausting plane trips to medical specialists, and a total disruption of his calling and ministry. I fear that if I had been forced to walk his pathway, that rain would have stopped play, and I would have given up, at least on hope.

I first met Eric Gaudion 300 years ago (or so it seems) when we attended the same Bible College. His smile is what I remember most. Eric is one of those natural, warm gentlemen; he was always destined to be a quality Christian leader. What was not on the radar screen back then was the battle that he would have with his health. I recently met up again with Eric and his wife Diane in their home in Guernsey.

Eric tells the truth about pain. There's no gloss, fluff, hyper-spirituality or clichés. The absence of them all makes me grateful, for slogans sting like salt on an already deep wound when you're suffering. You won't find slick answers in this book, or a satisfying, 'they all lived happily ever after' ending. What you will find are words that are written in blood, sweat and tears rather than just ink. You'll look into the heart of a fellow traveller, who must have been tempted to slam the door once and for all in the face of a God who calls himself good. Here is warm hope, honest empathy, faith that is gritty and authentic.

Read these words, and you'll find yourself humming along with Paul and Silas as they bellow out their hymns into the midnight darkness. Open this book and you'll find yourself in the company of Job, who was so pummelled by life but refused to throw a punch at God. Eric's words are like a lighthouse on the bleakest Guernsey day.

Eric Gaudion knows how to sing in the rain. Surely his lilting chorus will be a lullaby of comfort to some, a stirring anthem of bravery to others, and a whispered summons to worship – whatever the weather – to yet more of us.

May God bless you.

Jeff Lucas

Preface

I have written this book in four parts.

In Part One, I share insights into my own decade of pain. I do this to try and give you a sense of being there and of understanding the perspective from which I write. This is not an attempt to seek sympathy – your own story may be far worse than mine and I know that many go through even more difficult circumstances all the time – rather, it is an attempt to draw back the curtain and let you see inside some of the experiences that have formed the rest of the book. It offers the inside track on what it feels like to come very close to death on more than one occasion. It faces many challenging questions like 'Where is God's love in our suffering?' with no slick or easy answers.

In Part Two and the shorter Part Three, I share hard-won insight into how we can survive storms in the Christian life without becoming bitter, and how we can go through suffering and yet glorify God in our trials. In Part Two, I deal with things that can hinder and things that can help. Then, in Part Three, after taking a brief look at Job, I concentrate on Paul's storm in Acts 27, examining how the 'storms' of our lives, whatever they may be, can actually serve to make us more effective followers of Jesus Christ. What are your storms? Opposition, sickness, pain, personal failure? I hope you will find comfort, strength and encouragement in your personal struggles as you read.

Part Four is a challenge to the church to face up to the needs of suffering people in their congregations, especially those for whom healing is delayed or even denied. Church should be a help, not a hindrance in times of pain. This section should be of special interest to sufferers and their carers, but also, I hope, to my colleagues in ministry and Christian leadership.

Eric Gaudion, Guernsey, Autumn 2006

Part One

Nothing is Wasted

Introduction

...we are not ourselves
when nature, being oppressed, commands the mind
to suffer with the body.
(Shakespeare, *King Lear*)

Pain.

Blinding, searing, tearing, grating pain.

My fingers grope for my stomach, as if by magic I can stem the lava flow of agony. It feels as though a crazy workman is using a blowtorch on my abdomen. Will he never stop? What is he going to do next? Will I be killed?

In the long hours that lie ahead, there is a slight ebb and flow of the pain, but only the tiny neap tide of the most inconsequential change. I am in the grip of agony.

Along with this consciousness of pain there's a growing urgency inside me – I want to tear at the array of tubes and wires that protrude from every orifice. It feels like some of them have made new outlets of their own... and they have. Drain tubes stick out of my stomach at right angles to my skin, reminding me of a beer keg as they flex slightly, filling with fluid and then sloshing it through to waiting bottles. The pain is making inroads into my ability to think straight.

Denial. This isn't happening to me.

Then comes the voice, tart and stern.

'You're not in pain, Mr Gaudion. You've got an epidural!'

At this, my memory throws up a picture of the anaesthetist telling me that I would be largely pain-free after the operation because they were going to put in an 'epidural'. What's gone wrong, then? Why am I clawing at my midriff like a man trying to rid himself of something evil that has just sunk its fangs into his side? Suddenly, I'm aware of a sound – a child, screaming in distress... a child so close that they must be in the bed right next to me. The pathetic cries bring tears to my eyes.

'Stop making such a noise, Mr Gaudion, you'll disturb the other patients!'

It hits me with force. That primal howl – it's not a child. It's me.

But I'm forty-five years old. I'm a 'together' kind of guy. I'm also a Christian pastor. Under normal circumstances I would have been in this hospital on official pastoral duty, ready to offer comfort and prayer. No way would I ever willingly wish to disturb the peace of desperately ill people; I'm usually very thoughtful about that kind of thing. Also, naturally I am the very last person to howl and scream when in pain, preferring to go into a deep silence than let people know how I'm feeling. But right now I want to yell out, 'I spend my life doing my utmost to minimise the distress of others! I don't go around trying to add to it! You think I'm doing this *deliberately*?'

Instead, I hear myself pleading, 'I'm in such pain!', begging for understanding and relief.

The Intensive Care nurse in charge of me glances my way. Her voice is cold. 'I don't think you are, Mr Gaudion. Just breathe more deeply and relax.'

Through the pain, I realise there is an element of nursing philosophy at work here. By reminding semi-conscious patients that they have an epidural anaesthetic following surgery, the nursing staff intend to give subliminal comfort and relief. (Later, I reflect on just why it should be necessary to remind them of this if the thing is doing its job. Surely the relief such a device gives should be self-evident, even if not immediate?) In my case, though, I *know* the epidural isn't working, reminder or not.

Eventually, thankfully, anxious nursing staff call in the consultant anaesthetist.

'Oh dear. I think you're still in pain, aren't you?' Her voice is kind; a gentle Scottish lilt. Relief floods me.

'Thank goodness someone understands!' I gasp. 'Can you do anything about it?'

'Aye, of course we can. I'm not going to leave you until your pain is under control. We'll set up a PCA for you – that's patient controlled analgesia. Then you can use it to press a hand-held button and inject yourself with morphine as and when you need it.'

'But isn't there a chance that I'll overdose... or become a drug addict?'

'Not with this form of pain relief. The device limits the amount of drug being injected so that it's not possible to overdose. This is a highly effective means of controlling severe pain in the post-operative setting, and it should help you. In fact, research has shown that when patients are given such a device, they usually give themselves much less morphine than they would otherwise have been given by injection.'

I don't need any more wordy explanations. I'm only too pleased to be quiet and let her get on with it. I don't realise that I'm going to become uncomfortably familiar with such devices. Morphine and other opiates are to become a part of my life as I battle with pancreatic pain, night and day, with very little relief, for nearly ten years.

But my relief is only surface deep. Inwardly, I'm tormented. Because the real question nagging away in my mind is: 'Have they found something sinister... do I have cancer?

1

Before the Storm

This terrifying series of events happened during my *annus horribilis* – 1997. Of course, I didn't know then that this wasn't the beginning of the end of pain; in fact, there would be years and years of suffering to come. Indeed, searing pain would become a constant companion and an unwanted guest at every family milestone and celebration. Things had certainly not been like that up until this point, and I had mostly been a fit, healthy, enthusiastic participant in the game called life.

Born in Guernsey in 1952, I was the middle brother of three. My older brother by two years struggled with learning difficulties. This meant that through most of my childhood I was responsible for keeping an eye on him. When I think back, it feels as if Alan was always there with me, and I felt a heavy responsibility for his safety and well-being.

This may have contributed to my having an 'old head on young shoulders' and being given other responsibility at a young age. I became head boy at primary school and a young prefect and sports captain at the public school to which I was given entry by scholarship aged eleven.

I had no real interest in spiritual things during most of my childhood, dropping out of Sunday school once I was old enough to be self-conscious and nervous about performing in any kind of celebration of the Christian year. It also seemed incredibly dull and boring to me; I loved the active life. I was someone who enjoyed playing in the open air and swimming in the sea. I had a great respect for people with faith, but found it hard to feel sure of any such thing myself; I wasn't 'a believer'. When all the boys in my year were required to be confirmed in our Church of England-based public school, I asked to be excused as I had nothing to confirm – other than my confusion about what exactly was going on during the Anglican ritual to which the whole school was subjected on a daily basis.

The first stirrings of my awareness of the claims of Christianity came as a result of being required to be present in the school chapel one Good Friday. The drama department were putting on a passion play out of sight behind us up in the organ loft, so that the whole school listened to the events of that first Good Friday portrayed in sound only. I sat through most of it unmoved, until the awful moment that the wrists and ankles of Jesus were nailed to the cross. When the mallet thudded into the metal, something jarred my heart. I felt the dreadful unfairness of what was done to someone who only seemed to want to help others and was doing no harm to anyone. I left the building profoundly unsettled in my mind, wanting to know more about the mystery of this man's life and death.

Some time later, I was in Guernsey attending the sixth form college, when I was invited to church by a friend at the rifle club where I went shooting. Within three weeks of first attending (mainly drawn by an interest in the girls in the choir!) I found myself once more confronted by the message that the death of Christ on the cross was deeply significant. This happened when I went to an after-church evangelistic meeting at an Elim church. And so it was that I accepted Christ as my Lord and Saviour on a freezing January evening in 1968 and was 'born again'.

My life took on a change for the better. Suddenly, instead of partying on a weekend and drifting aimlessly from one week to another I felt I had purpose and goals in my life. I joined a gospel music group called Soul Enterprise and we set about telling other young people about Jesus. I began preaching and was amazed to discover that people actually became Christians as a result of what I was saying. Soon, I felt that God was calling me into Christian ministry.

I was still quite interested in the choir girls, though, but all that stopped when I met Diane Guille. She was the organiser of a young people's group treasure hunt at church, and I confess, I was smitten from the start. I loved her radiance, her laugh... I thought she looked *so* enchanting and attractive with her curly brown hair, natural smile and twinkling eyes. I remember that during refreshments time, she offered me some soup and I realised my chance had come.

'Yes, I'd love some please. Um... I didn't quite... catch your name?'

'Diane with one n – Diane Guille.'

'Oh, I know some Guilles! What's your dad's Christian name?'

'Wilson. Wilson George Guille.'

She didn't realise I was only after the initial so that I could locate her in the phonebook!

I found out later that Diane had been praying 'Lord, please don't let me be left on the shelf!' She was all of sixteen at the time! She had seen me before, at the evangelistic meeting where I had made my commitment to Christ, and had said to the Lord, 'That's *exactly* what I've been looking for! Please arrange for us to meet!' So we did. We became 'an item' and have remained inseparable since that day.

My call to ministry meant a two-year course at Elim Bible College (since renamed Regents Theological College) at Capel in Surrey. Following graduation I was appointed as an assistant pastor at Eastbourne Elim Church, assisting the then president of the Elim churches, John Lancaster. Six weeks after arriving at Eastbourne Diane and I were married, and began a pastoral ministry that was to see us serving churches in Weymouth, Whitehaven (Cumbria) and Delancey on our home island of Guernsey. Diane entered into the work of being a pastor's wife with real trepidation. She has always fulfilled the role with great ability and grace, although I know she has never been comfortable with the title of 'pastor's wife' and the expectations that often accompany it.

Our only son Matthew was born in 1981, and five years later we felt that God was calling us as a family into missionary service. We moved to the Seychelles, a wonderful chain of over one hundred islands in the middle of the Indian Ocean to work with FEBA Radio (Far Eastern Broadcasting Association). I threw myself into the work of a missionary broadcaster with great energy, travelling widely in India, Singapore and East Africa gathering material for programmes and setting up leadership training initiatives by radio.

In 1990, following a year's furlough, we moved to Zimbabwe to work with Elim International Missions where for three years I was engaged in leadership training and church planting, together with drought relief and oversight of the national Elim churches. This was another busy period, when my generally good health and robust constitution were great assets as I travelled widely within the nation and beyond.

When Mr Mugabe's government decided not to renew my work permit and visa, we had to leave a country that I in particular had really come to love. Our leaving was softened a little by an invitation from our old friend and mentor John Lancaster to join him on the pastoral team at the City Temple in Cardiff and then to become its Senior Pastor upon his retirement.

Little did we realise when we moved to Wales in 1993 that just over three years later we would leave again under very different circumstances.

2

The Path of the Storm

My life at Cardiff was a busy round of study, appointments, visiting, leading committees and driving around the hectic traffic lanes of the city. I was involved in counselling, preaching and leading worship. I loved it all, even if it left me very little time for family life or rest. Generally speaking, apart from some back problems, I kept well.

My battle with illness began in the October of 1995, when I had difficulty in doing my work because of central abdominal pain, weakness and nausea. This had just crept up on me over a long period. I started taking a lot of drugs for pain, and copious amounts of anti-indigestion medicine. At first I just presumed that it was all merely a sign of stress. I determined to try and take more time over my meals and to slow down a little in general. After a while, though, I found that I was growing tolerant of the many different kinds of antacids that I was taking. They were simply not having the effect that they had done initially. After one course, I was getting no significant relief. When I visited a chemist to ask if there was any other brand that I could try, he refused to sell me any more unless I went to a doctor. Wise man.

Things were getting worse. Waves of incredible weakness would just wash over me. In seconds, without warning, all my strength was gone. Frequently I found myself sitting on the windowsills of one of the terraced houses which surrounded my city centre office, trying to summon up the energy to walk on to my car a few hundred yards away, or get back to the office. Sometimes I would lose all my strength in a public meeting, when addressing hundreds of people. Mostly I coped with that by sheer effort of will, but on at least one occasion, I collapsed very publicly in the pulpit with great embarrassment all round. I knew that I needed help.

The first visit to my doctor resulted in a referral to a specialist. When my GP heard my story, and examined my abdomen, he realised that I would need further investigation. He suspected a gastric ulcer was to blame for my symptoms. So began the long road that led to an understanding of my illness.

***

One of the problems I faced throughout the early stages of my battle with illness was that it took a very long time to reach a diagnosis of my condition. There were many reasons for this, but the delay resulted in a long drawn out process of pain and frustration. Really, one of the first steps required in coping with pain is knowing what is causing it. Once the cause is known, then the vital next step of 'owning' or recognising the reality of the pain can be taken more easily.

Under the National Health Service in Great Britain, the whole procedure of getting help takes so long; it seems all the more so when you are in pain. Each test, even simple X-rays, means around at least six weeks for the test to be booked, the procedure undertaken, the results to be forwarded to the doctor, and a follow-up appointment booked in order to get the results from them. When a whole series of tests are needed in order to make a diagnosis, as in my case, this can all take ages. That does not even take into account the whole problem of waiting lists. The longest wait is often getting to see a specialist for the first time. For me that process was cut short by an emergency admission to hospital. This constant waiting can often have the effect of sapping a suffering person's hope, yet hope is absolutely vital to process of hanging in there, and recovery.

Time, of course, is of the essence in the case of chronic pain. In fact, the very definition of chronic pain is that it goes on for a long time.

> Chronic pain is often ill defined as to the source or cause; lasts longer than three months; and is commonly associated with multiple biological, psychological, and sociological consequences...A variation on chronic pain is chronic intermittent pain, that is, pain-free times alternating with weeks or even months of daily pain.[2]

This is a helpful definition of chronic pain, or chronic intermittent pain, but the reality is still almost unbearable. The biological, psychological and sociological consequences mentioned above began to hit me for six. I began to discover that pain isolates the sufferer. I used to seek out places where I could just be alone for a few moments and try to get control by breathing deeply. I lost concentration so that I could not even read. This was especially sad because reading was something that had previously been a central part of my life. I had no desire to go out anywhere for social reasons. I only went to places that I was really obliged to go in order to fulfil my duties, but I began to cut myself off from normal friendships and social events. This is not unusual for the person in agony. Here's how a girl called Philippa put it. She was a photographer suffering from sciatica, originally caused by a slipped disc

> The biggest effect [of chronic pain] is social isolation. You don't believe you can go out and meet people any more. You don't believe you have anything to offer them. In a sense, your pain becomes your identity. There is nothing else to speak about. All your experience is about pain and being in bed surrounded by four walls. It becomes a self-perpetuating cycle.[3]

Another major issue for me at the beginning of my struggle with pain was my increasing inability to do my work. By this stage, Pastor Lancaster had retired and I was the Senior Pastor in the church. The congregation numbered many hundreds of people, and many more were connected to the fellowship through the network of youth clubs spread around the city which were sponsored and staffed by the church. It soon became apparent to me, and to those I worked with, that I could not go on much longer. Long periods of sick leave were given, and then passed without change. Invariably, I would start back to work, doing well only for the first few days. Several times, after a period of leave, I preached with great fervour and blessing. People thought that I looked well. On many of these occasions the congregation burst into spontaneous applause when I appeared on the platform. Yet the longed-for recovery was not to be. Within a couple of weeks the picture would change. I had no stamina.

I simply could not continue in my ministry much longer under those conditions. Those to whom I was responsible within the denomination were concerned. They came to visit me to see if there was anything they could do to ease my load. It seemed inevitable that if my physical weakness continued, I would have to relinquish my post – a thought that appalled me.

It was decided to operate on me to remove my gall bladder and a quantity of gravel-like gall stones that were present. Everyone hoped that this would be the answer to my problems, but it turned out to be just a *bend* in the road and not the *end* of the road.

Worse was to come.

Despite having been a very healthy person for most of my life up until then, some months after surgery to remove my gall bladder, I entered into what can only be described as a harsh explosion of out-of-control, 'in your face' pain. I didn't know it then, but this was pancreatitis, a serious medical condition that can be life-threatening. It causes a pain that is difficult to describe. All sense of reality outside of the pain itself recedes. The whole process of thinking subsides. Animal instincts surface; the sufferer just curls into a foetal position in a despairing attempt to survive just a moment longer against the relentless agony.

I faced (and in fact, still do face) the doubting expressions of others constantly. I understood why they denied the reality and the extent of my pain – I did too. I was hard on myself, reasoning that it must be 'all in the mind'. I berated myself for my lack of moral fibre. Frequently I pressed beyond my pain threshold, ignoring the screams of my pain-racked abdomen, to do things that were neither necessary nor helpful, all in the name of 'gritting my teeth' and overcoming. As it would be unmanly to admit my pain, and perhaps lacking in faith too, I soldiered on, hoping all the time that it would just go away. It did not.

People who were praying for me meant well, but greeted me with exasperation when I told them the truth about my ongoing pain.

'That just cannot be!' they protested. 'We're all praying for you.'

'Well, please don't stop!' was all I could think to say.

It was (and is) hard enough to suffer the pain without being asked to explain why I still had it. Worse still, imagine the added weight that is piled upon someone already reeling under such a load of pain, when it is presumed that they are suffering because they lack the faith to be made well! That is a very cruel misunderstanding of Bible teaching and experience.

Failing any idea of what else to do, my doctor recommended that I take six months complete rest to see if that would give me time to recover. Whilst I agreed with that decision, and could see no viable alternative, it meant giving up a wonderful opportunity for ministry in a work that I loved. It also meant that we would have to leave our tied house so that a successor could be appointed. The idea of moving house when in such a state of ill health seemed ridiculous, yet, given the circumstances, I had no real alternative.

These were some of the serious repercussions of pain in my life and family. Not that my experience was unusual. Chronic pain affects the ability to work and lead a normal life. There are, of course, financial implications too. Incapacity Benefit is little enough, but in my case I did not even qualify for that because during one of the vital qualifying years I had been working abroad in missions. Thankfully, the denomination stepped in to maintain my salary, but I am aware of many who are not so well taken care of. Pain is no respecter of rank, status or profession.

Throughout our period of need, God's people have been faithful in their giving to us. Diane and I have truly seen the fulfilment of the precious promise of God to 'meet all your needs according to his glorious riches in Christ Jesus' (Phil. 4:19).

This promise, however, does not make the Christian immune from trials of both a physical and a financial nature. The issue is whether we trust God in the middle of those trials.

A good friend of mine was an active and much-loved headmaster. He was also a keen sportsman and long-distance runner. Suddenly, after years of keeping his body in fine trim, my friend fell victim to a particularly cruel form of rheumatoid arthritic pain. The levels of pain that he endured were harsh and at times unbearable. He still looked fairly well, and could not put his pain down to what other people might consider to be deadly serious illness like cancer but he was, nevertheless, devastated by his situation. This went on for months, with him doing his best to function in an important job, whilst fighting his own war with pain.

Like me, my friend looked to God for his healing, and continued to trust him come what may. Eventually, despite his best hopes and expectations, he was forced to face up to the inevitable. He recognised that in his circumstances, he could not go on doing his demanding job. His only pathway was clear, and he took early retirement from the post he loved (*very* early actually). I understand something of the sense of loss and grief that he must have felt, and the frustration of having a career cut short by pain. But then, pain never comes alone. Social life, finances, employment – *all* are affected, and that can be almost as bad as the pain itself.

This guy remains a close friend, and his courage and faithfulness in his suffering have been an example to me and to others. But then, one day his pain just began to lessen; it has now left him altogether, so that he has been able to do some supply teaching and is leading a schools evangelism ministry. So, that particular trial did pass. He and his family have been through a fierce test, yet they have continued to trust God and give him first place in their lives. Their story has been an encouragement to me and shows that Christ meets his people's needs, though not always in the ways that we would like.

The months before I gave in to the inevitable and stepped down from my full-time post passed in a haze of pain, weakness and disappointment. Endless hours were spent in hospital outpatient departments. Long weary periods of boredom were punctuated by brief moments of activity when nurses would come to weigh me, or ask for a urine sample. Then we would get our big moment with the specialist, who would be surrounded by cohorts of trainees. He once introduced me to them with the words 'Ah yes, the man with the interesting abdomen!'

I knew that things were getting pretty bad when he started seeing me without the entourage, in a side room. It was almost as if I had become an embarrassment – an oddity to be kept from the eager students in case they become discouraged! The tests went on, each one worth six weeks on the calendar, and roughly nil on the diagnosis score. At least we were ruling out everything from bile duct cancer to bilharzia. (Remember, I had worked in Africa. Always good for a try!)

Occasionally, I would meet members of my church in the waiting rooms. Often they had been through the same surgery as me, and were doing fine!

'Thanks for your prayers, Pastor!'

'We're thinking of you!'

Then, with a light pat on the arm they would be off towards the exit, glowing at their clearance from the doctor, and the glorious 'answer to prayer' that they had received.

What was happening to the prayers for *my* recovery? Had they got lost in the post?

I know now that they were heard, even before they were expressed. Even the thoughts and intents of my heart were known in heaven, and God was aware of my need. What I could not see – and perhaps my members could not see – was that God was answering the prayers very clearly, but not in the obvious way that we wanted or, perhaps, expected.

Throughout the whole period of this trial, my family and I have received scores of signs of God's provision and grace. The one thing we did not receive was the very thing we wanted so very much – my healing. But nonetheless, God showed us in amazing ways that he was with us. I may have been alone in some ways, but I was *never* isolated from God – even if sometimes I felt as though I was.

***

It was the saddest day of my life so far. The previous Sunday had been our farewell service at Cardiff and now I was sitting in the front passenger seat of a dear friend's car heading for Southampton airport. I had taken the doctor's advice and that November day in 1996, my family and I were setting off to our island home of Guernsey to begin what we thought would be a few months of sick leave. Still, I sensed that it might be longer than that before I would lead a church or fulfil my calling again and my heart was very heavy.

When we said farewell to our friends in the car park at Eastleigh, and turned towards the terminal building, I wept. Diane comforted me while our son, Matthew, walked awkwardly beside us. It just seemed so unfair. I had been at the very pinnacle of my career, serving God in a flagship church with an outstanding opportunity for preaching and leading a growing congregation, and here I was, heading for home... a broken man.

My overwhelming desire for active ministry was right and understandable given my gifts and calling. However, I was to find out that it is still possible to live for the glory of God regardless of circumstances. I discovered the truth of what John Piper, theologian and author of several books, has said: 'God is most glorified in us when we are most satisfied in Him.'[4] Because, although I have not been able to find satisfaction in relief or healing or indeed in as much activity and ministry as I would have liked, I know that Christ is sufficient as my Saviour and Healer. I have continued to try to keep my heart focused on him and his promises. It has not always been easy to do so, but I have found it is the key to inward peace in the most devastating circumstances. Back then, on that cold November day, I did not know this in reality; I did not know what was to come. I *hoped* that a few months' rest would mean recovery. But as I left Cardiff with my vision for the church undimmed, in my heart I knew that my own hopes for being a part of it were over.

Arriving back in the island soon put an end to any possibility that my symptoms were being caused by the stress of my busy lifestyle. It took only one interview with our highly recommended GP to convince me that the six months of rest theory was fatally flawed. He reviewed my case with an almost evangelistic zeal. His conclusion, following examination, was that if there was something wrong with me, and in particular with my pancreas, then all the resting in the world would not change that. He needed to find out more.

My new GP suspected that I may be suffering from an underlying chronic pancreatitis. He sent me to see yet another consultant gastroenterologist in order to have one further test done, an ERCP (endoscopic retrograde cholangio pancreatography). This is a special investigation for taking pictures of the bile ducts and pancreatic duct. It involves inserting a special flexible telescope into the mouth, down the gullet and into the stomach. It then goes into the duodenum opposite the opening of the bile duct and the pancreatic duct. A small tube is pushed through the opening, and a contrast dye is injected into the ducts. X-ray pictures are taken while the contrast dye is injected. Mercifully, patients are sedated during the procedure, and do not remember anything about it afterwards.

ERCP is safe with no complications in 95 per cent of cases. There are occasionally complications, the most common of which are abdominal pain, mild pancreatitis, biliary infection or bleeding. In very rare cases, acute haemorrhagic pancreatitis may occur, and because of this, occasionally death. ERCP is always performed by a specialist – and it is only ever performed for a very good reason. This test would be necessary I was assured, despite its risks, in order to confirm the diagnosis. It did also have the potential of being a cure if, during the test, any correctable problems were found and dealt with.

I did not agree to the test lightly. My wife and I were both, by that time, weary of doctors and hospitals. The test would also involve another gastroscope, and my previous experiences of this procedure were not very encouraging. I took advice from several friends and contacts, including doctors, some nurses and ministerial colleagues. It would have been preferable to me if the test was being undertaken in one of the several centres of excellence in dealing with the pancreas, perhaps Southampton or London, and not on our island home.

Finally I agreed to the test, and on 22 January 1997 I went into the Day Patient Unit of the island's hospital to undergo the procedure.

I did not return home that day. Instead, I finished up in Intensive Care... with acute haemorrhagic pancreatitis.

3

The Storm Hits

Someone was ill... very ill indeed. I could hear voices
– doctors' voices, low and concerned, whispering.

I knew I was in the Intensive Care Unit. I also knew
it was night-time, but not because it was dark. Day and
night were the same in the ICU, the only difference
being the voices of the staff were a little subdued at
night. It struck me as strange that there were doctors
milling about – usually the Unit was run by nurses
with the doctors just popping in and out.

Then I heard one of the doctors say: 'We're losing
him.'

Losing who? I didn't know, but I felt so sorry. In my
subconscious I whispered a prayer for the one who was
dying. What I did not know was that I was the only
patient in the ICU that night.

But as I prayed, I realised how uncomfortable I felt.
In fact, I could hardly breathe. It seemed to me that
they had turned off the oxygen supply, and I began to
pull at the mask trying to let the staff know that there
was something wrong with the flow. Frustrated at my
inability to communicate with them, I sucked at the
mask like a starving child attempting to suckle at the
shrivelled breast of its tragic mother in some African

drought. I did not know that my lung was filling up with fluid as I suffered the effects of pleural effusion, a complication of the illness that had put me in the ICU – acute haemorrhagic pancreatitis.

Fear was the main issue. I can remember similar feelings from my childhood when during nightmares I would lie in bed terrified, but unable to call out to my parents. In those times, I thought I could sense some dreadful monster crawling up my bed covers. I even imagined that I could hear the slight movement of a spider crab's legs (a popular form of sea crab eaten in Guernsey but not in the UK) crawling up my pillow. When I opened my mouth to cry out, no sound emerged! There was just a terrible silence, broken only by the rustling on my pillow. I think now that those noises were most probably made by my hair standing on end! The sense of impotence and loneliness that I felt then were worse than the fear of the creatures in my imagination. I croaked and cried under my oxygen mask, begging for air, but no one seemed to hear me. They stood around me as if I was saying nothing at all, and that my movements, sounds and gestures were part of some other world. Perhaps they were.

I was choking, and I could feel the panic around me, as well as rising within – but then, all of a sudden, everything changed. Peace came like an unexpected visitor and rested on my bed. For a brief while I was aware of an intense sense of comfort and the presence of Another. It was like what I imagine it might feel like to be in the 'eye' of a hurricane. After the terror and rage of the elements came quietness and a deep hush. All was still around me. I felt loved. I knew that I was no longer alone. I was surrounded in a comforting light that was not harsh like the fluorescent tubes above my head. In place of the familiar antiseptic smell of the

ICU and the plastic and rubber of the oxygen masks, I could definitely smell the fragrance of flowers and berries, just as if I was walking down a country lane again as I had done so often as a child.

At some point that night I felt as though I was on a journey, moving towards a distant light. As I did so, travelling by foot but not really walking – more floating – I came against a barrier, which seemed to me to block my path like a wall. It towered over me and I stood at the bottom of it, looking for the gate I was sure would be there. I could hear such wonderful sounds of music and laughter coming from the other side of the wall. When I say hear, I mean more than that really. I both heard and experienced the music. I felt the emotion of the music too. It seemed to me to be worship of the deepest kind that moves your soul and causes tears to flow. It soared in cadences too high for most human vocal chords and the harmonies reminded me of the natural blending of voices we often heard in Africa. The nearest I can come to describing it is like the experience of 'singing in the Spirit' you may have heard in some charismatic churches, where it seems as if an unseen conductor is leading the music while it blends effortlessly into a glorious and heavenly overture.

The wall was my problem. It seemed as if it were impenetrable, preventing me from going any further. Into my fevered mind came the most soothing voices.

'Don't worry Eric, it will only be a short way now, and then you will be home. We're here to help you.'

'It's only a short distance, Eric, and Jesus will meet you there, when you arrive.'

I was so amazed and relieved to be free of the terrible negative emotions of the recent days. It seemed as if someone had just turned off the switch marked 'evil', and turned on the one labelled 'love'. I felt calm and comforted in a way that made me think I was being hugged.

The experience did not last long. Obviously I did not make that final crossing, or I would not be writing about it today. I am convinced that I was near death that night, as was confirmed to me later by a male nurse, who served me with such kindness in the ICU, and whose assurance of his own prayers meant so much to me. This was as close to the moment of death that I have ever come, and it was an experience of great peace, and reassurance. I know, of course, that I will go to that place again one day, probably in very different circumstances. Then I will find the gate and enter through it. But I am not afraid. I have been there before, and I know all will be well. At least, in that sense, not everything that came out of that desperate time was negative. There would be at least one other occasion during my stay in hospital that I came to the brink of death, but this one stands out in my memory for the sheer contrast of light versus darkness. It was my moment of truth. For some reason, unknown to me, I was spared, perhaps due to the prayers of my loved ones.

***

Telling you about this near-death experience is not easy. I do not enjoy recalling the events of that terrible time. Doing so has fixed one or two firm convictions in my mind.

The first is that it is so important to deal with the issue of death while we are still alive and well. I was only in my forties when all this came upon me, unbidden and without warning. Others face even greater trials at a much younger age, and some are spared till later. One thing is certain, however, and that is that we will all die, and face eternity. Being ready for death is at the very heart of the Christian faith, but it must not be taken for granted. We need to know that we are ready. During the two years prior to writing this, I have been back into hospital sixteen times and had seven surgical procedures, each one carrying a high risk of complications that could cause death. Each time I have been in hospital, someone near to me in the ward has died while I have been there. These are pancreatic biliary units, and the men there are all desperately ill. In it all, Diane and I have been granted opportunities to speak with some of them about our faith, and we count that a real privilege. Hospital chaplains do a great work, as do visitors, but when they have all gone, and men are lying side by side in agony from the same complaint, then they tend to get down to the nitty-gritty! Being a sufferer has given me unique authority to speak to fellow-sufferers, but at a high price.

I will never forget the example of a very dear friend of mine, Steve, who died of malignant melanoma in his mid-forties, leaving his wife and three children behind. His courage and faith were an inspiration to many. When asked how he coped with being terminally ill, he would often say, 'We are *all* terminal.' In that way, he urged people to be ready for the day of their own passing.

I only came to a place of certainty about the reality of what goes on after life here on earth in my teens. I made a commitment of my life to the Christ of the gospel, and have never again doubted that when I die, I will go to be with him. Jesus himself said: 'I tell you the truth, whoever hears my word and believes in him who sent me has eternal life and will not be condemned; he has crossed over from death to life' (Jn. 5:24). When it very nearly came to it, my faith was very much confirmed by what I experienced. How people cope with the kind of thing that I went through – and far worse – without the knowledge of Jesus in their lives, I just do not know.

Secondly, I have become even more convinced that we need to think seriously before we make any moves at all towards the legalising of euthanasia. I have the greatest sympathy, as one sufferer for another, with anyone who longs for death as a way out of intense pain. Yet, in the ICU, all the time that I was unable to communicate with the staff around me, I was terrified that they might do something to end my life before time. If I had filled in any kind of 'living will' beforehand (such as is suggested by the supporters of voluntary euthanasia), I know that I would have regretted it then. I even rued the day that I had placed an organ donor card in my wallet, and hoped that the ICU staff were not aware of it! It seems to me that one great problem with the 'living will' idea is that the patient may change his or her mind and yet not be in a position to do anything about it. During that terrible time in the ICU, I absolutely dreaded that the medical staff, perhaps seeing me as a nuisance, might try to end my life in order to get rid of me. It was not that I was afraid to die; quite the opposite – the experience I've described was sufficient to end that fear. No, the issue for me was two-fold. I could not bear the thought of leaving my wife and son before time. It was especially painful for me to contemplate my teenage boy growing up without his dad. Also, I did not want to be killed. Everything within me was fighting for life, however flimsily. The thought that one of the staff might, by carelessness or design, hinder me in that fight, was more than I could bear. Thankfully, they were all on my side, and my fears were only delusions. That is as it should be. In my opinion, for a doctor to be asked to become a killer is a hideous breach of trust. I hope that this country's laws will always protect the rights of the unconscious and the vulnerable.

My brief but close encounter with death was to become just another step on this pilgrimage of pain. It had significance for me, though, far beyond the time it took, or even the experience itself. It made me aware that I was actually not alone in my suffering, but that God was watching me. It left me with the sense of having been hugged. More than anything it enabled me to say to myself that if I do lose the battle and die, all will be well.

But my near-death experience wasn't the end of my suffering in the ICU. I was by no means 'out of the woods' yet.

4

Battling the Storm

The air around me was tense with confrontation. Only two nurses remained in the Intensive Care Unit along with me. I had been too ill to be moved when everyone else was evacuated. My body was fixed to too many lines, monitors and tubes. I could hear negotiations going on by radio between the nurses and the police outside. It was clear that time was getting short. The bomb could go off at any minute.

I could see that the explosives were hanging in a black haversack suspended about five feet from the ground on the wall opposite my bed. Wires connected to the power circuits hung menacingly from the package. The black bag beeped and clicked occasionally, causing me to shudder with fright. I had never known such fear in all my life. It was bad enough being so sick that I had been confined to the ICU for I didn't know how long, but now I was embroiled in a deadly serious terrorist plot!

Why was this happening? The nurses were no real help to me, so I had to work it out for myself. I believed that one of them, a male nurse with a beard, had been discovered earlier in the day stealing morphine from the Unit's locked drug cupboard. My suspicion was that he was in league with a gang who were supplying opiates for sale on the streets. Once this nurse had been discovered, he fled. Later that evening he returned, carrying his cache of explosives, and laid siege to the department. The deal was that if he and a female nurse accomplice were not allowed to escape in a helicopter, together with their haul of drugs, by midnight, they were going to blow the Unit sky high – and me with it!

I longed for the police to grant their demands, but it seemed unlikely. Finally, as midnight approached, I was allowed to say goodbye to my wife over the radio. I knew it was the end. Filled with dread, I drifted into oblivion.

To my amazement, I was still alive in the morning. Once my eyes focused again, the relief I felt was beyond words. The bomb was gone! The Unit was functioning again. There were no more signs of terrorist activity. But it was difficult to understand why the nurses were not rejoicing that we had survived such a traumatic night. They went about their duties in their ordinary fashion. I decided that it must be due to their desire to cover up the bad publicity that such a story would bring if it got into the newspapers!

I know now, of course, that the terrifying ordeal of the bomb plot was just one of the horrific fantasies that tortured my mind during the three weeks I spent in Intensive Care with acute haemorrhagic pancreatitis. The hallucinations were caused by a mixture of opiates, oxygen deprivation and blood poisoning that was going on inside my body; the paranoia was a direct result of my condition combined with the powerful drugs being used to save my life. The black haversack which I really believed contained the explosives was actually a TV monitor tracing my vital signs. The only opiates being taken out of the drug cupboard were for me! But to my drug-soaked eyes, it was all so *threatening*.

For days after the 'failed bomb plot' I was convinced that I had personal police protection. I thought that there was a surveillance unit above the ceiling panels, watching me and the surrounding area through ventilator holes. I *knew* the young man in the next bed to me was not sick at all. He was an agent with Special Branch. So was one of the porters. I kept giving them knowing winks. I even muttered to them about 'ward security' and the safety of visitors. All this was taking place as I floated in and out of consciousness.

Not that the bomb incident was the only threat. I spent most of that period in a state of extreme paranoia, convinced that the staff and other patients were plotting to kill me. On at least one occasion that deception proved so strong that it took several nurses and a doctor to restrain and subdue me. They narrowly prevented me from pulling out all the drains and lines in my screaming frenzy and desperate attempts to escape from the bed.

Another time I became convinced that they had thrown me out of the Unit, bed and all. I imagined that my bed was standing on the grass outside the main hospital entrance! This delusion was so convincing that I can remember actually feeling the drops of rain falling on my face.

It became difficult for me to know where I was. My tortured mind invented transfers to other hospitals and various medical evacuation flights, all in an attempt to keep me out of the way of the terrorists. On one occasion, convinced that I had been flown to a hospital in Northern Ireland (perhaps because of the terrorist link in my fevered brain), I was amazed to see my wife Diane and her friend Sandie come through the door to visit me. I was so touched by their devotion that they had been willing to travel all that way to stay near me.

In another delusion I fantasised that a physiotherapist, whom I took to be a special agent, had moved me first to a nursing home and then to her own home for my safety. During all that time I never actually moved from my bed in the ICU.

I will try never to use the word 'paranoia' in jest again. It describes such a terrifying, lonely condition. I can now feel the utmost sympathy with anyone suffering from paranoid delusions – for whatever reason. It was a terrifying side-effect of the battle to save my life. Strangely, as I reflect on that whole period, I can recall very little of what *really* happened to me. The fantasies, however, are all deeply imprinted on my mind. At times of weakness or pain they return to frighten me... a sort of flashback which I hope will diminish in time. Without doubt, the weeks that I spent in Intensive Care, and the months of recovery which followed it, were the most painful and harrowing of my life.

I can see now that there was an all-out satanic attack on me at that time. My view is that the enemy's intention was to silence my ministry by trying to kill me, and that certain demonic powers were capitalising on my frail state. I have no desire to get that out of proportion, but nonetheless believe it to be true. However, I know that my heavenly Father has to give permission for anything to touch my life. This was revealed in the experience of Job, who was afflicted only because God gave Satan permission to do it (see Job 1:6–12).

During all that desolate time, as I was battling with the powers of darkness in the ICU, believers were interceding for me. Several of them received revelation that there was a direct assault of the enemy on my life. Diane heard from the Lord, a word based on Luke 22:31–32. Here Jesus was speaking to Simon Peter, of course, prophesying his denial, but Diane put my own name into those verses. Then it became very personal, and very powerful, especially in the Amplified Version

> [*Eric, Eric*], listen! Satan has asked excessively that [all of] you be given up to him [out of the power and keeping of God], that he might sift [all of] you like grain, but I have prayed especially for you [*Eric*], that your [own] faith may not fail; and when you yourself have turned again, [*or recovered – my own addition*], strengthen and establish your brethren.

When wheat is sifted it is normally cut down first, and I had certainly been cut down! So, the battle raged, as it did with Job, and the shell-blasted battlefields were my mind and my flesh.

I was impressed with the way that Job was able to see the overruling hand of God even in the middle of such awful physical and mental suffering. Knowing that fact for myself helped me greatly, but as I passed through those dreadful weeks, the battle was very hard indeed. The writer of Psalm 119 says: 'It was good for me to be afflicted...I know, O LORD...in faithfulness you have afflicted me' (Ps. 119:71,75). But it was difficult to hold on to those truths.

I did not die in the ICU (obviously) but there were times when it seemed to me that death would have been preferable to what I was going through.

When the time for some relief came, strangely it was quite sudden. Diane tells me that one Sunday she was saddened by the obvious distress I was in, despite the large amount of pain relief still being given intravenously.

In all my time in the hospital unit I had been fairly vocal. I often cried out to the Lord for help and deliverance. When they were doing things to me that

I found frightening, I would call out the name 'Jesus'. On other occasions, I would speak in tongues (see Acts 2:4), sometimes at the top of my voice! One doctor turned to Diane and said, 'Is it true you spent time in Africa?'

'Yes,' she replied.

He nodded. 'I thought as much.' He believed I was speaking in an African language.

From that Sunday morning, however, I began to scream very loudly indeed, and continued to do so for thirty-six hours. I did not know what was happening, although in my subconscious I could hear the staff trying to ease my obvious discomfort and get me to breathe more easily. I just could not stop making this dreadful noise. It was as if something deep within me was yelling out. Some of the staff had seen this before, but others had not. Some held to the theory that some deep inner distress was surfacing – a catharsis – and perhaps it would be for my good. Despite the disturbance that I caused to the ICU and the nearby operating theatres, they decided to allow this to continue and to subside naturally. Actually, they also dared not sedate me for fear of suppressing the only indicators that were keeping me alive. So, I screamed on. Diane found this so disturbing that for a couple of days she felt unable to visit.

During that time, remarkable prayer was happening on my behalf. People were fasting and praying, in the UK and overseas. Others were praying through the night for me (and I am humbled and grateful for their love and care). When I finally became silent – my voice gave out completely and left me unable to speak for some days – the worst had passed and my pain began to recede.

When Diane saw me the following Tuesday (incidentally, a day of concerted and intense prayer for me among friends, especially at the church in Cardiff where I'd been the Pastor), she could see my pain had lessened and I was quiet. She asked the staff what drugs I was now receiving for pain, and they simply said that I was not at that point on *anything* for pain.

Romans 8 tells me that creation groans in its fallen condition, that we groan as we long for the deliverance that the Lord's return will bring, and that the Holy Spirit groans when he prays through us prayers that are in the will of God. Perhaps some of that groaning was happening in me during those long hours of crying out. I don't know... but at the end of it, I was much calmer.

***

I don't want to exaggerate the negative side of my experiences under the influence of the drugs and the illness, but it remains very vivid in my memory. I find it sad to have to admit that throughout the period of my stay in the ICU most of my fantasies were negative and frightening. As a Christian I try to fill my mind with good things, and steadfastly avoid violence and evil in the media, and also in life as much as possible. Yet, in the Unit, I was frequently oppressed by fear, paranoia, confusion, horror and vulnerability. I was later told that these were the results of the drugs and toxins in my body but as I have said, I also believe there was a supernatural or spiritual dimension. I felt hated, threatened, forgotten and alone, despite the wonderful reassuring presence of my lovely wife who came every day, and mostly twice daily, to sit by my side. Often my mum and dad came too; sometimes my

mother came alone, and some close friends called in as
well. In fact, Diane recalls that for the space of around
ten days I did not know her or my parents at all. I was
present physically but deeply unconscious and just not
aware of people, fighting my own inner battles with
darkness alone.

When it came to the major surgery that I was to face
some months later (and about which I wrote in the
opening pages of this book) I told the anaesthetist my
story. She was glad that I did, as, bearing those facts in
mind, it enabled them to plan my pain-control regime
on that occasion. Thankfully, the psychological problems
did not recur. Perhaps the particular mix of toxins and
opiates that had been present to cause me problems at
that time did not come together again. All I know is
that there are worse things than pain. Sometimes the
price paid for relief is so high that you have do some
bargaining, trading sanity for relief, or vice versa. But
it is important not to keep quiet about the disturbing
side-effects of some drugs.

5

Coming Through

After three weeks in the ICU it was felt that my condition had improved enough for me to be moved back on to the general ward. Soon, after weeks of 'nil-by-mouth', I was allowed to take my first faltering sips of water. My dream over several days had been to go to a country pub with my friend Bob, and order a pint of ice-cold water! I longed for the sheer delight of allowing crystal-fresh water to trickle down my parched throat. During the long period of intravenous feeding, I had only been allowed to have occasional teaspoonfuls of crushed ice. They had been as delectable as the tastiest morsel. But now, I could gorge myself on 30 mls (about a tablespoonful) of water per hour! What luxury!

Once I was keeping that down, it was possible to graduate to clear fluids on demand. The day finally came when it was announced that I was to have my first cup of tea. I remember that a wonderful nurse named Chris made a big fuss of preparing tea for Diane, our friend Sandie, and me. They had each been given a cup and saucer, while I had a plastic 'birdie cup' with a spout, usually given to babies and geriatric patients! When, later that day, my parents came to see me, Chris repeated the whole tea party occasion for them too. It was such a joy for me to share those moments with them. The only problem was that the tea, milk and sugar tasted like poison to me. I was to learn in the next few days and weeks that it takes ages for the taste buds and digestion to come back to normal after the kind of assault to which mine had been subjected. Still, I was now a tea-drinker.

But it was a long time before I could eat normally again. Hospital food did not agree with me. I loved the look of it and the smell but could never get it down in any quantity. It was like chewing sand, and swallowing was such hard work. However, once I was home again, Diane set out to tempt me like some gastronomic seductress. Tiny platefuls of attractive morsels were waved in front of me. Anything I asked for, or showed any interest in, was obtained and lovingly prepared. Mealtimes were dreadfully hard for a long while, but gradually, slowly, more and more real food slipped down. Eventually, I started to eat normally again, though not in the quantities to which I was used. I doubt if I will ever be able to binge on food again, as I am quickly full (but that will do me no harm – I have always erred on the podgy side!).

Anyway, thanks to dieticians and a loving wife I was back to relatively normal eating. Even the nearly three stones of weight that I lost in hospital returned to me in remarkably short time. The initial effects of weight loss upon me in the immediate aftermath of the ICU were devastating. For many patients in the ICU, and especially with pancreatitis, the loss of weight is mainly due to protein being lost – muscle weight. It was estimated that when I left hospital in an emaciated condition, I had lost between 50 and 80 per cent of my muscle weight. A high protein diet and gently increasing exercise was required to recover from this.

Chronic pain, however, was to return with a vengeance, and the surgery of which I spoke at the start of this book followed six months after my stay in the ICU. And that wasn't the end of it; my ministry was destined to be framed by bouts of agonising pain. On my better days, I could function quite well, and I did have a few prolonged spells without having to take very strong relief.

After two years of rest and recovery following the major pancreatic surgery, I began to serve God again as a pastor in Shiloh Church. They were kind enough to call me as their team leader at a time of growth in the church, which has continued to see God's blessing in the years that have followed. Of course, I could never be sure of being well enough to be at an event or a service, and needed occasional times of rest. Up to this time, when we have envisioning days or retreat times at a local Christian centre I always book a nearby bedroom so that I can sneak off and rest. (However, one of the benefits of the Senior Pastor not being as strong as he would like to be is that many members of the church have had the opportunity to grow in their own ministerial callings. We have a remarkable staff of full-time and part-time pastoral and administrative people. The church is also mobilised into teams that function in very efficient ways, relieving the leadership of much of the burden.)

Then, early in 2004, it became necessary for me to take sick leave for a prolonged period again as pancreatic pain rose to a crescendo and the morphine I needed made it impossible to drive or to preach. Over the next two years I was admitted to hospital many times both in Guernsey and in central London, often as an emergency. I have twice been transferred by ambulance and air to London from Guernsey with ambulances taking me to the plane and meeting me at Gatwick. Several dangerous procedures with high risk of causing life-threatening complications were performed in that period. And then I discovered further major surgery was required.

***

'What a waste of time and effort!' That's how Diane and I feel about a period of prescribed total pancreatic rest and an enforced forty-day fast. During the six weeks or so before the major operation that I had in August 2005, absolutely nothing would pass my lips, not even a sip of water. I knew that the impending surgery was necessary, and that the surgical team was insisting that I needed to rest the pancreas beforehand. This meant that I was fitted with a tube which went directly into my jejunum, a part of the small bowel, bypassing the stomach completely. I was allowed to rinse out my mouth with mouthwash, but not to swallow anything at all.

This enforced fast was as difficult for Diane as it was for me. We have always been a close couple, and have taken all our meals together for the more than thirty years we have been married. If we have a cake or a cookie we always divide it in half, and being together for meals is a must in our busy schedule whenever it can be achieved, despite the many demands of the ministry. Now, all that had to change.

'I'm becoming a secret eater!' Diane said, sadly. 'I don't want to have cooking smells in the house that will tantalise you. Sometimes I even sneak outside to eat in the garden!'

'I'm so sorry, my love,' was all I could find to say. And I marvelled once again at the self-effacing sweetness and kindness that have always been the marks of her contribution to our relationship.

In the end, my situation became so dire that I was readmitted to hospital, severely dehydrated and suffering from ascending cholangitis. It was unclear as to whether the harsh regime had been of any real medical benefit. But was it a waste of time? Was I simply the victim of medical experimentation or a well-intentioned mistake? Was the agony worth anything?

Romans 8:28 may be one of the most often quoted – and perhaps misquoted – verses in the Bible: 'And we know that in all things God works for the good of those who love him, who have been called according to his purpose.'

Yet, if those words are true, they mean that no experience that a Christian goes through is wasted. During my enforced fast, I was often also in great pain. Sometimes I just couldn't think straight, because of the effects of morphine on my system. But I spent a long day thinking seriously about a remarkable part of the Old Testament that I had often previously overlooked. And I felt that God was speaking to me!

It all began when I was reading Romans 9 and came across these words in verse 13: 'Just as it is written: "Jacob I loved, but Esau I hated."' This passage brings up all sorts of questions about why God chooses one and not another (and of course it is all about his grace in showing mercy to those whom he will show mercy) but it was not that age-old theological sparring subject that caught my attention. No, I was struck by the fact that for 400 years, if you had asked the descendants of the one whom God loved whether this verse was true or not, they would probably have laughed in your face! While the descendants of Esau (Edom) were enjoying their hill country inheritance and relative prosperity, the offspring of Jacob were spending 400 years in slavery in Egypt, courtesy of God's chosen servant Joseph. That is the equivalent of the people of Britain being enslaved from the year 1600 until the twenty-first century. That's a long time! Can you imagine how the Israelites felt during those long years, which started well but just got worse and worse? Being God's chosen favourite is no bed of roses.

Yet God was at work in the slave quarries of Egypt. He was turning a family into a nation. He was preparing a people who would be desperate enough to accept the delivering leader Moses, just at the right time. For the final eighty years of their enslavement he was preparing their deliverer in the wilderness, long after he must have thought that any hope of being used by God was gone. When the time came, the people of Israel (Jacob) were crying to the God of their fathers.

The relationship that God had with his enslaved people was built upon a blood covenant, made by God with Abraham in Genesis 15. In verses 13 and 14, He even told Abraham that his descendants would become slaves in a foreign land for 400 years and that He would deliver them. As Christians, we are also in a relationship with God based upon a blood covenant, made with the blood of God's own Son on the cross. The New Testament says that we too will suffer in many different ways in this life, but God does not waste our sorrows. Everything we go through, however dark, however long, serves to make us more like that which God wants us to be.

Therefore we do not lose heart. Though outwardly we are wasting away, yet inwardly we are being renewed day by day. For our light and momentary troubles are achieving for us an eternal glory that far outweighs them all. So we fix our eyes not on what is seen, but on what is unseen. For what is seen is temporary, but what is unseen is eternal. (2 Cor. 4:16–18)

Truly we can say, with God nothing is wasted.

Conclusion

Recurring acute pancreatitis is one of the most painful conditions known to humanity. Pancreatitis is an illness of the pancreas which produces various symptoms, the most difficult of which to bear is the pain. Though the intensity of that pain goes through cycles, it is always there. Pain is like the 'neighbour from hell' who will not allow you to develop your own garden. Instead, he challenges every plan you have, dashing every hope. Attacked constantly within your own private areas, your creativity withers and eventually dies under the onslaught. Energy is sapped.

Since falling ill, everything I have done has been beset by pain. I have sought relief by a variety of methods. From prayer to opiates, TENS machines to deep breathing, exercise to rest, I have tried them all at one time or another. Being involved in healing ministry myself I have had hands laid on me by various colleagues with proven track records. I've cried out to God. I've fasted. Whenever I have heard of a healing meeting where there are Christians seeing miracles and breakthrough, I have been there if it was at all possible. I have received prayer from some of the biggest names in Christendom. So much oil has been poured upon my head it's amazing my hair ever dries. But as one who has seen people healed in response to prayer, I have to admit, for me, it hasn't happened.

But in all this, I have continued to preach when able, to minister to people in the hospital wards, and have gone on trusting the God who loves me and could heal me, but seems to have chosen not to do so – yet.

During this decade of agony I have learnt many lessons along the way about coping and just hanging in there as a Christian, even when it would be easier to scream than to pray. Now, let me share those lessons with you.

Part Two

Things That Hinder, Things That Help

Introduction

It is amazing how the number forty appears again and again in the story of God's dealings with men and women in the Bible. There were the forty days and nights of Noah's rain, Moses' forty days on Mount Sinai, Elijah's forty days of strength from one meal, Nineveh's forty days of repentance following the ministry of Jonah, and of course the forty days that Jesus spent in the wilderness being tempted by the devil. In addition the church which we have the privilege to serve and be a part of has recently been greatly strengthened and encouraged by being part of Rick Warren's well-known Forty Days of Purpose programme and its follow-up Forty Days of Community.[5]

Forty days became significant for us as a couple when I underwent the six weeks of 'nil-by-mouth' treatment as a total pancreatic rest in preparation for some more major surgery in 2005. There was nothing to satisfy the hunger pangs and above all the thirst that marked the whole forty days. In an effort to make the enforced fast bearable, I offered it as a 'fast to the Lord' and tried to be open to hearing the voice of God during this difficult time.

Medical fasting, however, is very different to the spiritual discipline of fasting. For a start, there is no real sense of being called by God to undertake the fast in the first place. I was taken by surprise when the rigorous regime was put in place, with little or no warning and certainly no preparation. Secondly, overwhelming weakness, hunger and thirst, and constantly feeling cold despite it being the height of the British summer made concentration on prayer and reading difficult. Also, apart from the ongoing sense that all was not well, there was the fear of the forthcoming surgery and the question of whether I would survive it or not. Altogether a very different picture from what I have always imagined a forty-day fast might be!

What this period of forty days did do for me, however, was enable me to review some of the lessons that I have been learning through all this long decade of pain. This is by no means all that I have learnt, but what follows should provide you with insights into suffering that will be helpful and faith-sustaining in the midst of trials of all kinds. Thankfully, not too many people in the UK or the USA will ever experience the horrors of acute or chronic pancreatitis, but whatever your trials are – whether in body, mind or spirit – these principles will help to pull you through.

I've called this section 'Things that Hinder, Things that Help', and I hope that by reading it, you will be strengthened and encouraged.

1

Things that Hinder

The Stiff Upper Lip

I realise that there is a cultural issue at work in the whole area of being real and owning up to one's true need. I believe the British people have been locked into a long, loveless marriage with stoicism. (Stoicism is a system of belief and practice that calls upon its followers to accept their lot in life with serene detachment. Therefore, a 'stoic' is a person who suffers great difficulties without showing his or her emotions.) This union has at times run sweet, then sour. It served us well during the terrible wars and deep depressions of the last century. The famed 'stiff upper lip' saw the nation and its peoples through many years of dreadful suffering.

Yet even in dark times of conflict, the marriage between the British people and their philosophical outlook was beginning to crack. Strain showed in the trenches during the Great War, where terrified young men, suffering (as we now know) from post-traumatic stress disorder, were executed by their own comrades for cowardice. A large number of British troops were sacrificed to the ignorance of that time, and the demands of 'keeping up morale'. I could cite other instances where this obsession with morale-keeping showed itself in more than one cruel way. I am sure you could, too.

However, I believe I understand the dilemma facing the 'old guard'. I am of Scottish descent, born into the Guernsey island race. Our national characteristic is stubbornness. This is so much the case that island people are known colloquially as 'Guernsey Donkeys'. My old public school motto was *Semper Eadem*, literally 'Always the Same'. Change is difficult! Typically for my generation, I was brought up to believe that it was weak to weep. We all loved each other fervently in our family, but nobody ever dared show it in any demonstrative way. Long after I had married and moved away from the island, the thing I hated most about revisiting our home was the knowledge that I would have to find an appropriate way to greet family and friends on arrival and departure. I just felt so awkward, not knowing whether to shake hands, or grab hold of someone, or God forbid, even kiss them. On departures, my heart was breaking inside, but I did not dare let it show.

Thankfully things *have* changed, and in keeping with the emotional revival that is sweeping our nation, I now just grab hold of my loved ones and hug! You know, those moments of touching someone can mean so much. At least when I lay in the Intensive Care Unit, on the brink of death, I knew that my mum and dad were aware that I loved them because I had recently told them so, and vice versa. Just a few years before, that would not have been the case.

So, the marriage is over. The British people, on the whole, want their divorce from stoicism. No divorce, of course, is ever clean. There are always conflicting opinions pulling in different directions. Because the British now find it acceptable to 'open up' a bit more, they perhaps 'open up' to dubious practices. One problem is the abundance of 'counselling' as a spin-off from the new emotional climate. Whereas once people would have kept their emotional pain to themselves, now they seek out counsellors. The law of supply and demand means there is a plethora of willing, though sadly not always very qualified, practitioners just waiting to serve all sorts of needs. New Age practitioners abound with all their weird and wacky answers to life's problems. Personal life coaches (whose own lives may have been a litany of bad choices and breakdown) offer their services to help others change their lives... at a price.

At one time, the parish priest would have served as a father confessor to whole communities. Nowadays vicars can be portrayed in the media as at best irrelevant, at worst part of the problem instead of the solution. There is a lot of money to be made from counselling, and many dangers involved. A psychiatrist friend, dubious about the amount of counsellors in the church, once said to me, 'Never open any door you cannot close, or expose any wound that you cannot heal!' Whilst we should not lose sight of the value of counselling in times of pain, we must beware the marketplace with its tendency to plunder the desperate.

On the other hand there are some very good and godly men and (more often) women who are getting trained up and accredited to do a great job in the area of Christian counselling. Our own church has a whole team of folk who are going through such training and making themselves ready to meet some of the huge numbers of people who desperately need help.

Of course, it's the biological family that should offer real support. It does – when it's working properly. There ought to be an environment in the home where we can tell it like it is without being mocked and rejected. The home *should* be a sanctuary, a place of protection from the predatory forces of the outside world. Sadly, far from being a means of relief and care in times of pain, many families have become the *source* of the pain. The home is too often a place of conflict, and the uncontrolled expression of negative emotions. Yet in my own pain, I can only say that I found great relief in being able to 'be real' at home, and being believed by my family even when test results were all coming in as negative. I was not easy to live with. Pain does that to you. It makes you touchy and testy. But, if charity begins at home, then so too does the battle against pain. Being real about our feelings and our pain must begin with those closest to us.

For a long time I refused to listen to my wife's pleas to slow down and change my lifestyle. Would that I had listened to her! I was speaking to a crowd of several hundred people. Suddenly, in the middle of my talk, all my strength left me and I was engulfed in a red mist of pain. I stumbled to a halt, stung more by my embarrassment than the internal discomfort, and had to be helped from the platform in front of the concerned crowd. A doctor was present in the meeting, and explained to the people what was happening in my life. He told them that if I had listened to him I would not have even tried to address them that day. And he also told them (with my permission) that they wouldn't see me again until I had undergone an operation. What he said was so sensible, but my sadness and grief over 'letting the side down' knew no bounds.

Why do we afflict ourselves so? What insecurities within drive us to deny reality until it is almost too late? For what reason did I torture myself and my loved ones rather than admit I was in need? I don't really know the answer to those questions, but I am determined not to live that way again. 'Walk in the light' is sound advice that I have ignored to my peril. Whether by schooling, or by a false sense of manhood, or because of the pressure of the unspoken expectations of others, I was not walking in the light.

'Being brave' in the old-fashioned way is all right for a while, and perhaps serves as a way to get through short term crises. In the long run, though, bravery can only work if it is grounded in the kind of reality that owns up to what is really going on in our lives. It then becomes the strength to face the reality that we freely confess. Courage calls us forward against a named and known foe. Only cowardice would deny the facts. And perhaps that was my problem. The appearance of being brave and denying troublesome symptoms and gnawing pain was a form of cowardice – a running away from reality. Only when I repented of that cowardice, as I do now daily, could I begin to enter into hope and healing.

Maybe in that limited sense, my pain has helped me. It has certainly forced me to sort out my priorities, and to look again at the way I mistreated myself and my family in the name of busy-ness. There must be more to life than that. I think that even in my early consulting with doctors I was searching for a pill or a treatment which would take away my pain without requiring a change to my lifestyle. I was too busy to get well any other way. Discipline can prove extremely inconvenient. I wanted a quick-fix solution that enabled me just to get on with my life. I suspect that I am not alone in this.

Perhaps a large part of the doctor's role is to confront us with the unreality of this attitude. A number of doctors would probably say that many of the patients are coming to them only to find a way to carry on living the way they like without facing the consequences. I think *I* was like that. But it has all had to change. A lot of healing in my case has been to do with the re-arranging of priorities, and also with attitude. I had to learn what the apostle Paul meant when he said, 'We demolish arguments and every pretension that sets itself up against the knowledge of God, and we take captive every thought to make it obedient to Christ' (2 Cor. 10:5).

So, examine yourself. Do you suffer from 'stiff upper lip syndrome'? If so, I think it's time to say goodbye to your stoicism and be honest, either with your family, your friends, a trusted counsellor… or yourself. Don't you?

Sweet Rebellion

Cathy (not her real name) was a delightful young missionary, working in a European country. She had returned home to the church where I was serving as pastor in the 1980s for a short period of furlough, and she was a real blessing and encouragement to our young people. She was tall, elegant and beautiful and radiant with the beauty of Jesus. We thanked God that she had been home and sent her on her way back to the field with our blessing and our prayers.

It was over two years later that we heard that Cathy was home again. This time, she was living with a man who was not her husband – a man who had been married to someone else. He was not then a Christian. Diane and I went to visit her, just to express our love and to share our concern for her well-being. We were unprepared for what we found. The radiance was all gone. In its place was a worn-down, hangdog expression of someone with eyes averted, hiding from us and from the world. She stopped attending church for quite some time, until thankfully, many years later her walk with God was renewed and her new partner, then her husband, came to faith in Christ.

When we left Cathy's home that day, we parked on a nearby headland and wept. We wept, not just for the tragedy of so much lost by that dear servant of God, but for the rebellion in our own hearts. Yes, the Holy Spirit used that example of overt rebellion to expose the hidden rebellion in us. We call it 'sweet rebellion' now – the state of being where everything looks so holy and spiritual on the outside, but where inside we are raging against God and the world.

All rebellion is obnoxious to God, whether it's hidden or open, sweet or sour, and it leads to loss in our lives. The Bible is clear about this. After all, rebellion was the original sin of Adam and Eve as they set out to disobey a simple challenge given to them by the Almighty. 'For rebellion is like the sin of divination, and arrogance like the evil of idolatry' (1 Sam. 15:23a). Serious stuff. But when *believers* rebel, we often have to cover it up pretty well so that our Christian routine can continue. That is 'sweet rebellion'.

> Woe to him who quarrels with his Maker, to him who is but a potsherd among the potsherds on the ground. Does the clay say to the potter, 'What are you making?' Does your work say, 'He has no hands'? Woe to him who says to his father, 'What have you begotten?' or to his mother, 'What have you brought to birth?' This is what the LORD says – the Holy One of Israel, and its Maker: Concerning things to come, do you question me about my children, or give me orders about the work of my hands? It is I who made the earth and created mankind upon it. My own hands stretched out the heavens; I marshalled their starry hosts. (Is. 45:9–12)

One aspect of sweet rebellion is an unwillingness to accept the will of God for us or the way God has made us. Now, of course, we all regret things we have said and done that have grieved God and others; we also regret the effects of ageing. But that's not what we are talking about here. Sometimes Christians suffer unnecessarily from their own sweet rebellion when they avoid the mirror – or even look disdainfully into the mirror and dislike what they see. Other times we look longingly and begrudgingly at some other Christian leader's success or charisma and long that it might have been us. For some – and for me, this is a tough one – pain or disability drives us to question what God has made and to doubt the work of his hands. It may be sweet rebellion, because no one else knows. But *God* knows and *we* know. It's a form of idolatry or even an attempt to control nature and circumstances. And that, of course, is much the same as divination.

The only answer to sweet rebellion is the same as for any kind of rebellious sin. Repentance – a turning around to walk in a different direction. Let's be honest here. It won't go in a day. It needs to be a daily choice to rejoice in the Lord and the works of his hands. Psalm 139 can be a great help as we remind ourselves that we are 'fearfully and wonderfully made'. Quiet trust means that we lean on God's loving intentions towards us and believe that he is working for our eternal good.

Certainly, when all the distractions of food and mealtimes were removed from my life for many weeks, and hunger, thirst and pain became daily companions, areas of sweet rebellion were revealed in my heart. Choosing not to stay there is a daily discipline, but one that brings peace and rest. I wonder, are you in sweet rebellion? If so, I encourage you to talk to your heavenly Father about it now.

Rejection

Since the Garden of Eden, humankind has felt a keen sense of being rejected. This has come about because of the Fall (Gen. 3) and the subsequent banishment of Adam and Eve from God's presence. It has created a God-shaped vacuum in the human heart. Rejection and the fear of rejection can torment us at different times in our lives, but especially during trials and difficulties.

We have a dear female friend who is a pastor with a special anointing of the Holy Spirit on her life. She is widely regarded as having a close walk with God and when she stands to minister in public, whether in song, preaching or in praying for folk – the evidence of God's blessing and power on her is very real. Yet she has struggled with tremendous rejection in her life. From an early age she has known what it was to literally flee for her life when her father took his family away from their home country in order to survive the very real danger of political assassination. Yet the greatest battle that our friend has had to fight with rejection has come more recently during her Christian ministry and has been the result of the appalling way that she has been treated by fellow-ministers and Christian workers. Whether due to her ethnic roots, her gender, or just plain professional jealousy, she has suffered untold rejection by those who should have been her closest friends and greatest support. These things ought not to be. Yet, since Jesus first came to those who were his own 'but his own did not receive him', there have been unwelcome replays of this heartbreaking tragedy. When you are already going through a time of personal suffering or trial, rejection piled upon rejection is the last thing you need. But how do we cope? What resources exist to enable us to survive?

One tactic that can help us to hang in there against the undermining nature of rejection is the knowledge of who we are in God, and what he has already done for us – the security of knowing the Father's love and care. The Authorised Version translation of Ephesians 1:6 is 'To the praise of the glory of his grace, wherein he hath made us accepted in the beloved.' This is the bedrock of our desire to do God's will. He has accepted us in Christ. Knowing this is an antidote to rejection and the fear of rejection. The awareness that we are accepted by God because of his love and grace overcomes our insecurity. We are no longer victims of circumstances. Father loves us and has a plan for our lives.

But rejection and the fear of rejection are powerful forces. Since humankind was first driven out of Eden, only to find their way back barred by an angel with a flaming sword, the deep-seated fear of rejection has been very strong – a primal force. Hell is the final outcome of rejection. The harsh reality is that those who reject the Lord Jesus Christ – God's offer of reconciliation and the way back to something even better than Eden – will find themselves rejected in eternity by the One who is the only source of life. But for the believer, there is the prospect of living a life of acceptance both here on earth and afterwards in heaven. This means both God's gracious acceptance of us in Christ, but also our joyful acceptance of God's will for our lives. The one springs from the other. We accept because we know we are accepted.

Jesus was able to delight in doing his Father's will because he was sure of his Father's love. He felt the constant acceptance of his relationship with the Father, no matter what was happening to him here on earth. Even during the awesome rejection and brutal beatings preceding Calvary, Jesus knew he was accepted by his

Father. He was 'rejected by men, but chosen by God, and precious to him' (1 Pet. 2:4). It was only on the cross that Jesus felt the cold blast of rejection by God. All the sin and rebellion of the world was poured onto Jesus as he became our atoning sacrifice. It was no longer possible, for that brief time, for the Father to look upon his son, because he had become sin – for us (see Hab. 1:13a; 2 Cor. 5:21), and an awesome rift appeared in the Godhead. In the agony of isolation, Jesus cried out: 'My God, my God, why have you forsaken me?' In that dreadful cry of dereliction there is evidence that in the incarnation, Jesus tasted everything that belonged to being human, even rejection by his Father in heaven. Thankfully that gulf was bridged by the very death that he died. Christ was raised from the grave, and now we can enjoy the sheer exhilaration of being 'accepted' in him.

It can also be a great help in the battle against rejection and the insecurity it brings, to take a Bible concordance and do a Bible study on all the uses of the words 'adopted', 'accepted', 'chosen', 'precious' and suchlike that are found in the Word of God. You will find that most of them refer to you! When we realise that we are of *immense worth* to God, we grow in the certainty that he will not leave us to our own devices.

We don't possess much that is of real value in our home, but anything that is special to us is placed where we can keep an eye on it. Increased value equals increased attention as far as we are concerned. God is just like that in his dealings with us. Whoever touches you touches the apple of his eye.

I would like you at this point to take a moment to reflect on this truth. And then go and find that concordance!

Fear

People are very afraid today. Fear is endemic in our society, as Jesus prophesied it would be in the last days. 'Men will faint from terror, apprehensive of what is coming on the world' (Lk. 21:26).

There is possibly no greater fear than when your own life is on the line. One of the most frightening things is to be seriously ill and to know that in order to get well you are going to have to get a lot worse and suffer a great deal. Some people face this when confronted with the spectre of chemotherapy. For me it was facing the likelihood of more radical abdominal surgery being required when I had already had so much. Yet fear is stalking those who are perfectly well and have nothing immediate to be afraid of. This is because of some of the things that are 'coming on the world'.

On Boxing Day 2004 I was stuck in a dismal hotel room in central London having been discharged from hospital on Christmas Eve, too late and too ill to get a flight home in time for Christmas. Yet my own worries became as nothing as I watched the news unfolding on the television screen. Thousands of Western tourists had been enjoying the ultimate escape – a holiday on a tropical beach instead of a freezing Christmas at home. Suddenly, their idyllic world was shattered as the earth was shaken along a fault line at the bottom of the Indian Ocean. The resulting tidal wave was devastating.

This following on the heels of the terrible events of 9/11 in New York 2001, when two aircraft crashed into the Twin Towers, bringing death and sudden destruction to thousands, some of them the wealthiest workers in the finance industry. Then, there was our own 7/7 in 2005, with the London bombings. Consequently, there is a sense that nowhere is safe from the upheaval that is in the world. The nations are certainly being shaken in fulfilment of Haggai's ancient prophecy (see Hag. 2:7).

Fear and worry

Fear is a powerful force in its own right, whether the thing feared comes to pass or not. But it soon becomes clear from a reading of the Scriptures that fear can be linked to several issues in our lives. There is a link, of course, between fear and worry. Jesus taught about worry in his preaching ministry, something so practical and down to earth that the crowds were delighted and challenged by his words: 'Don't worry about your life, what you will eat or what you will wear – don't worry about tomorrow.'

We recently inherited a tiny vase from an aunt of Diane's. It has pride of place in our kitchen and on the side is written the words 'Do not burden today's strength with tomorrow's cares'. Jesus put it another way: 'Therefore do not worry about tomorrow, for tomorrow will worry about itself. Each day has enough trouble of its own' (Mt. 6:34). Each day has its portion of problems and its own supply of strength. It never helps to use up today's strength before its time on issues which may never arise. When they do, our heavenly Father will give the needed grace at the time.

Fear and guilt

There is a link between fear and guilt. Right at the start of human history, when Adam sinned, he avoided God out of fear saying 'I heard you in the garden, and I was afraid because I was naked; so I hid' (Gen. 3:10). If we *knew* how much God loves us and what a wonderful and effective work of forgiveness Jesus has done for us, we would not be afraid through a persisting sense of guilt, but rather would come to the cross and let him deal with the problem of the sins we have committed.

Fear and lack of trust

There can also be a link between fear and a lack of trust in God. Luke 24 tells us about the disciples who were simply not expecting Jesus to do what he said he would do and rise from the dead. If they had only believed him, surely they would not have felt such fear (see v. 37).

At its heart, fear is a misunderstanding about the nature of God. God is good, and he plans good things for our lives (see Rom. 8:28). We need to choose to trust him.

Conquering fear

How can we conquer fear? Well, we need to choose daily to believe God's promises and reject the devil's lies. We need to read the promises in God's Word that combat fear (see the ten fear-fighting texts at the end of this book). We choose to believe his promises more than our fears or our symptoms. We need also to feed our minds on the positive things in life and not the negative. This means that we may have to ration our daily intake from the news media. When we lived in Africa, where at that time there was very little news to be had, we were amazed at how little we missed those daily bulletins of sorrow, sadness and gloom. We also missed the exciting bits too.

Another tactic for overcoming fear is to mix with others who believe God's Word. Their positive reinforcement of God's promises by their stories and by their prayers can really help us deal with our fears. Small group life can often be the means of great encouragement to believers and is highly recommended.

If we dare to call fear by its real name and admit that it is sin for a child of God to choose not to trust their heavenly Father, then we are embarking on a road to freedom. The first step in getting free is admitting we have a problem. The 12 steps of Alcoholics Anonymous acknowledge this. In much the same way, we can admit we are a) powerless over fear, b) believe God can restore us and c) make a conscious decision to turn our lives over to him.

Now we may not feel that an addiction to fear and worry is anything like as serious as many of the problems addressed by AA. But fear *can* be crippling (for example, agoraphobia – a fear of open spaces – can completely ruin the life of the sufferer) and worry potentially curtails our enjoyment of life. Still, whatever the level of our problem, once we admit it and confess it, we must not stop there. God has made a complete provision through the cross for our cleansing and freedom from all sin. We need to praise him for it – *every* time the negative thought comes back!

In all this we need to learn to lean on the love of God. 'There is no fear in love. But perfect love drives out fear, because fear has to do with punishment. The one who fears is not made perfect in love' (1 Jn. 4:18). When we realise how much God loves us then we shall put our fears to rest. He will do what is best for us. Then, whenever we are afraid, (and we will be because we are human), we make a positive choice to put our trust in him. 'When I am afraid, I will trust in you' (Ps. 56:3).

Doing it Afraid

Is there any way forward if all the fear-fighting texts seem to be ineffective against the fear? Yes there is. It is called 'Doing it Afraid.'

It's unusual for me to watch daytime TV. Perhaps being ill gives you an excuse, but it still feels uneasily guilt-making to be sitting down in front of the television when one should be working! Still, one day, I did glance at the TV – a Christian TV station, to be precise, an unusual event in itself. Now don't get me wrong, I have been blessed by watching some Christian television! Having been involved in the media as a radio missionary in the Seychelles with FEBA Radio during the 1980s, I understand its power. But some of it, I just don't enjoy. This day was different, however, because one of my favourite television preachers was on, Joyce Meyer. I like Joyce. She is clear about her own failings, and honest about her shortcomings. She was speaking about her ongoing battles with fear, and coined the phrase that I found so helpful, 'Doing it Afraid.' This little sound-bite gave me permission, as a Christian, to be scared. It gave me the preacher's blessing on the nervousness and fear of the unknown that nearly all seriously ill patients feel at times.

'Doing it Afraid' is how we became missionaries. In the months leading up to our move overseas after more than fifteen years of pastoral ministry in the UK, Diane and I were both very much afraid. We had, after all, signed a body release document in case we died overseas. We had made wills in which we had nominated some close Christian friends to become Matthew's guardians in the event that we might both be killed. All very cheery stuff when you are already leaving behind so much that is known and secure!

Added to all that was the very natural concern that we might just fail to be up to the job. In circumstances like these there really is only one course of action that makes sense. If you know that God has called you to go, and we had many confirmations that that was the case, then you choose to trust him and 'Do it Afraid.'

I have learnt similar lessons during my battle with serious illness. There is probably no lonelier place in the world than the anaesthetics room of an operating theatre where you have said goodbye to your loved ones and are waiting to be put under. In such a situation I usually try to remind myself of the promises of God. God has said, for instance, '"Never will I leave you; never will I forsake you." So we say with confidence, "The Lord is my helper; I will not be afraid. What can man do to me?"' (Heb. 13:5b,6) At times like that, the Psalms become very precious, and I find myself repeating the words over and over.

> He who dwells in the shelter of the Most High will rest in the shadow of the Almighty. I will say of the LORD, 'He is my refuge and my fortress, my God, in whom I trust.' Surely he will save you from the fowler's snare and from the deadly pestilence. He will cover you with his feathers, and under his wings you will find refuge; his faithfulness will be your shield and rampart. (Ps. 91:1–4)

I have found it helpful to memorise passages of scripture like this one. To assist in this I have written some of them out on cards, and placed them in strategic positions around the home. Another helpful tip is, I listen to music with biblical lyrics and tapes of Bible readings so as to help me when I am about to do something afraid.

You see, real courage is not the absence of fear, but the willingness to go on doing what we know to be right... *despite* our fears.

Disappointment

There's so much talk in the church these days about self-help that divine providence is seldom mentioned. But we do not *decide* God's plan for our lives, we *discover* it.

Much of the time we do not understand how God leads us. It is only in looking back that we see the big picture. Paul told the Romans that he planned to visit them when he went to Spain. But he never made it. Instead he finished up in one of Europe's worst prisons – but from there he wrote the Epistles. If we really believe that God is directing our steps, why do we complain so much?

One aspect of my painful trial that has been so hard to bear has been the sorrow of recurring disappointment. I got 'all prayed up' that the next surgery would fix the problem. But after the terrible pain and anguish in going through with it, the benefit would last for around three to four weeks... and then things would be worse than ever. It was hard to keep trusting when I was so disappointed, and also when I felt that I was the cause of so much disappointment to others – wrongly, I can see now, but not at the time.

We are too easily disappointed when our plans fall through; too easily discouraged when great career opportunities are missed. Our complaining reveals the fact that we do not know God like we say we do. Delay is often just the protective hand of a loving heavenly Father. One of my deepest disappointments was leaving Zimbabwe when the government of Mr

Mugabe refused to renew my visa. Yet if we had stayed then, my illness would have killed me three years later. Without the help of Western hospitals I simply would not have survived. God knew what he was about, and had a purpose in that frustrating and heartbreaking situation.

'Hope deferred makes the heart sick, but a longing fulfilled is a tree of life' (Prov. 13:12). I have certainly discovered the energy sapping power of disappointment over the years I have been in ministry. One of the very first experiences I had as a young trainee pastor was to minister to a family with two tiny children where the husband and father who was only thirty-two had been diagnosed with cancer and was not expected to live. We received so many 'promises' that he would be healed and a group of us waited expectantly by his bedside, even all through the last night that he was alive. His death was a shattering blow to my eager, fledgling faith. There have been many similar blows since, and amazingly some remarkable healings that can only be explained by the power of a loving intervening God who hears the cry of his children. Why not for *me*, then?

Obviously I don't have the answers to what are some of the fundamental questions of the Christian life – of why God allows suffering and why sometimes he heals and sometimes he does not. I am prepared to ask those questions when I get to heaven. Till then, I have found something to be true in all my painful personal experience: *Disappointments are sometimes his-appointments!*

For instance, I would not now be the pastor of the wonderful church where I serve if I had not been so ill that I was left with no alternative but to return in weakness to my birthplace. Like the apostle Paul I can

say 'As you know, it was because of an illness that I
first preached the gospel to you' (Gal. 4:13). Also, there
is no doubt that both Diane and I have grown in our
understanding of who God is and how he works in our
lives as the result of the terrible things we have been
through together.

On one of the many admissions to hospital in
during one recent year, there was a really strong sense
of disappointment in my heart. Yet, this visit was to
prove different to the others. There was an elderly man
opposite me who was being treated for cancer. My wife
and I made friends with this man, and so were able
to share the gospel with him. Diane was also able to
comfort the grieving mother of a seriously ill young
man from China in a nearby bed.

Then, a couple of pastor friends and their wives
came to see me in the open ward, and told me that
they believed the Lord had said that they should
worship him and sing with me. We drew the curtains
for some privacy, but privacy is one thing you don't
get in hospital. We began to sing quietly and in close
harmony 'Be still and know that I am God'.

The noisy ward became silent. Then there came a
shout.

'Do you take requests?'

'Yes!' we replied.

And, with the curtains still drawn, we began to sing
some of the pieces asked for – including 'All things
Bright and Beautiful'! Once the impromptu choir had
gone, one of the nurses thanked my wife and I for our
friends' visit, and said that our singing had moved the
entire ward – and could they come again soon?

So, as you see, sometimes our disappointments really
do turn out to be his-appointments.

But what if we are facing disappointments that don't seem to have any meaning? Nobody seems to be getting saved as a result of it, and maybe even the pain itself seems meaningless? Helen Roseveare asked a similar question when pressed to understand why God had seemingly deserted her during her appalling attack and rape at the hand of rebels in the Congo during her missionary service. Having recognised that God has planned his own suffering as a result of his immense love for us through the cross, she went on to explore a challenging personal perspective on her own suffering.

> So when I faced the horror of the shame and the cruelty of the guerilla soldiers, and God whispered to me, 'Can you thank me for trusting you with this experience even if I never tell you why?' He made it possible for me, by His overwhelming love, to accept the suffering.[6]

There is a classic Bible story that deals with the issue of disappointment in our Christian discipleship. It is Luke 24 and the story of the risen Jesus appearing to the two discouraged disciples who were walking to Emmaus (vv. 13–35). This was an occasion when the King of kings stopped whatever else he might have been doing on the first Easter day and went incognito to meet with two disappointed disciples. As they went along together, it soon became clear that the events of Good Friday had severely disappointed them. (Like them, I am also often disappointed when my hopes are not fulfilled. The suffering of life leads to situations that we cannot understand even if we know that we are doing the right thing, such as trying to be Christ-like or serving others.) One of the reasons why the cross had disappointed them so much, though, was that they had been holding on to some unrealistic and even false

expectations. They had read their Old Testament Bible
one way and come up with a set formula. Their reading
of prophetic scriptures meant that they expected that
the Messiah would overcome the rule of the Roman
invaders and turf them out of Israel. When their
formula failed, they were sunk. Jesus showed them
other scriptures that they not yet considered, scriptures
which foretold of the Messiah's sufferings and death.
We must always be wary of selective readings of the
Bible that produce simple formulae, especially in the
area of healing, where there are so few easy answers
and so much mystery.

The two disciples were also disappointed because
things had not worked out their way. They said 'we had
hoped' – but God was doing something different which
was not their way but his. 'As the heavens are higher
than the earth, so are my ways higher than your ways
and my thoughts than your thoughts' (Is. 55:9). God's
plan, for instance, for the great hymn writer Fanny
Crosby was that a doctor would give her the wrong
medicine when she was a baby, resulting in her total
blindness. Rather than growing bitter, Fanny Crosby
allowed her condition to make her more spiritually
sensitive; she wrote some of the most beautiful hymns
we once used to sing.

What the two disciples needed to understand was
that their story was not over. What they had seen so far
was only a fraction of what God would yet do. And we
need to see this too. If God is who he says he is – and
is therefore infinite and eternal – he does not have to
explain himself. If we could understand him and all his
ways, he would no longer be infinite, which by its very
definition means always one step beyond anything we
can grasp.

Ultimately life will always disappoint us, unless our eyes are on a faithful eternal God who never changes – and who is not a disappointment. So, believe he is directing your steps.

Isolation

One of the oldest tricks in the devil's book is to isolate suffering Christians from other people. I felt it happening to me on more than one occasion, yet I am a public figure, well-known in my congregation and community. How much more difficult must it be for sufferers who are not so well-known and integrated to maintain relationships and social contacts when their pain goes on and on?

I have worked hard through this period of suffering to try and maintain a level of communication with others that I could cope with. I have used the internet, with its emails, weblogs and communications software to keep in touch with people even on the other side of the world. The telephone is a lifeline and I am not beyond phoning up and asking the right people to pop in and see me briefly. I suppose I have an advantage there in that they probably feel guilty about refusing that kind of invitation from their pastor, but you should try it too. Waiting for the whole world to come to you is a very unhealthy by-product of years of immobility when there are many new methods of communication that can help us.

Isolation can cause spiritual and social starvation, and a withering of hope that comes through spending too much time alone without the nourishment of human fellowship. That's why it is so important for people in pain to resist it, and to do everything possible to try and maintain contact with others. It is also why those who care for us need to do their utmost, even by phone, email, text or letter, to assure us that we are not alone and that we are thought of often.

The warning signs of isolation can still be present, though, even when we are the recipient of visits or contacts from family or friends. We must avoid seeing ourselves as the centre of the universe and must really try to engage with others about what is going on in *their* lives. Asking questions about them and listening carefully to them will help to make people want to come and see us again. If the experience is a positive one for them then there is more likelihood of them wanting to repeat it. The occasional letter or card of encouragement sent by us to someone else passing through pain or difficulties can also keep us from being forgotten and be a means of enabling us to reach out to others despite our own needs.

If others do fail us in this regard, and leave us on our own, let's try and avoid the trap of bitterness. The Bible teaches us that the root of bitterness can spring up and adversely affect many people, and I have found that when I am in pain it is harder than ever to avoid it. Yet, when I find myself thinking things like 'He doesn't care or else he would have phoned by now', I have to take my feelings in hand and remind myself that I don't know all that is happening in his life and must be willing to make allowances. Most people who have not known real pain or chronic ill-health simply don't understand how it feels, and they can hardly be blamed for being busy with their own lives.

I often have cause to thank God that he doesn't forget me. He is my heavenly Dad and does not throw me away just because I'm broken or in pain. His presence and the comfort of the Holy Spirit have stayed with me through every attempt by the devil (or others) to isolate me. So, I'm *never* really alone. And if you know him, *you'll* never be alone, either.

Self-pity

Feelings of isolation can lead us on to self-pity. But it isn't easy *not* to have an attack of the 'poor me's when you are suffering.

But the fact is, there aren't many people less attractive than those who are constantly whingeing and moaning about their lot. The whole world revolves around them, and they are always the centre of their own attention. Yes, self-pity is a very real temptation when you are feeling low; pain with discomfort, poor diagnosis and all the other concerns that come with illness pile pressure upon pressure. But I have found that the price I pay for feeling sorry for myself is way too high.

Self-pity will turn us into a permanent state of victimhood if we are not careful. The question should not be 'Why me, Lord?' but rather 'Why not me?' God will use us in the storm of our suffering if our hearts can be kept free from self-pity. But how do we do it?

Well, first of all we need to see how *others* are suffering. We are not alone in being human and enduring the price of growing older or of being harshly treated by life. I have already spoken of how important it is to keep in touch with others and ask how *they* are getting on. Another benefit of taking the focus off our own suffering and trying to take an interest in the lives of others is, of course, that they are more likely to want to maintain contact (although that isn't the primary reason we show concern for others). And we must remember that self-pity isn't a very attractive trait, so assaulting a rare visitor with a stream of how awful our lives are may result in that person not particularly wanting to visit again, which of course leads us into more self-pity. Quite a vicious circle. Now, I am not suggesting we deny our pain. We must be real. But we have to sometimes look outside ourselves and our own suffering.

Another survival tactic is to try to avoid self-pity by seeking out even some small mercy in the middle of the situation that we face. I must admit, at times, the attempt to do this by others has become a real source of annoyance to me. I have poured out my trouble to a trusted friend only to be told something like 'Ah well, at least the weather's not too warm for you to be in hospital'! Well, several months earlier it had been. So, I think this technique of seeking out the tiny glimpses of grace in dark places is best left to the sufferer themselves rather than something that is imposed upon them by well-meaning but usually quite fit onlookers.

Wherever you find stinging nettles in nature, you usually find dock leaves growing alongside them. When we were children we used to rub the dock leaves on the stings straight away as they act as an antidote. The trouble is, when you are in pain, it's not always easy to see the dock leaves. I have made a choice to try and do so. Will you?

Unhealthy dependency

One of the most aggravating factors for Christians in the midst of difficulty is an undue reliance in, and dependence upon, the medical profession, good and helpful as they may be.

The position of the doctor in Western society has changed dramatically from what it once was. We have already considered the fact that at one time, people would have taken their personal problems and confessions to the parish priest or vicar. Nowadays the doctor, and in particular, the general practitioner, has become a kind of father confessor to the community. It is almost as if health has become a religious force in its own right, and the medical men and women its priests. Inevitably, when we are in pain, we look to the medical profession for help. We expect our doctor to be able to give a name to the pain. We anticipate that they will be able to discern the hidden meanings of the pain, and then to give us relief. If that is not the case, then we at least expect that they will be able to refer us to another doctor who can. This means that we are looking outside of ourselves for answers, and to a certain extent, we are surrendering responsibility for our recovery to the professionals.

This is all well and good if we are dealing with simple matters that can be easily rectified. When, however, long-term pain or chronic disorders are the problem, there is a subtle danger in the relinquishing of our responsibilities. We can start to see ourselves as passive recipients of treatments rather than active participants in a programme of healing in which both patients and practitioners are joint partners. We can also become so submerged in the paraphernalia of medical care and practice that we lose sight of God and his benevolent care of us. I certainly found that pain, drugs and the inevitable humiliations of hospital life clouded my vision of God's sovereign grace and power over me.

There was a time when there was an air of awe and mystery about the doctor; I think perhaps this was perpetuated by the medical profession itself. With a cry of 'Trust me, I'm a doctor!' I feel they reckoned that they, the high priests of medicine, always knew what was best for the patient and didn't like to be reminded of their limitations. One can still perceive today a touch

of arrogance in some medics but thankfully, not so much
as in days gone by. The 'Just leave it all to us, we know
what we're doing' attitude is quite unhelpful when
their patients find that after lengthy consultations and
programmes of treatment their pain is just as severe.

At this point, sufferers often become discouraged.
They imagine that they have exhausted every source
of help. What they have inadvertently done is to form
an unhealthy dependence on the doctors. When they
are 'let down' they can feel dreadful – totally bereft of
hope. Wise doctors do their best to remain humble and
accessible, always showing by their words and their
body language that they want to hear from the patient,
and that they do not necessarily know it all. (Wise
patients know that anyway.)

This unhealthy dependency can manifest itself in
many ways. Patients spend long periods dwelling on
every word spoken by the doctor, analysing every
possible nuance of meaning. They believe the 'oral
myth' – that is that there is some pill or potion which
will alleviate any ill. They spend their every waking
minute recounting the words and deeds of their medical
advisers to all who will listen.

'He said he had never seen one as bad as mine in all
his years in medicine, you know.'

Or, possessed of the certainty that doctors can fix
anything, they berate them for not doing so in their
case: 'He's just not doing enough for me.'

Such attitudes can be unhelpful in the process of
coming to terms with pain.

Let's try to remember that God made us so he knows
how to mend us. There are many pictures of God given
in the Bible that show him as a healing God. He is the
Great Physician. If any doctor deserves the right to be
trusted, he does. He calls us to trust in his ultimate

care of his children and to believe that even when the doctors reach the limits of their knowledge and can do no more, Dr Jesus is still in charge of our case.

It was so helpful for me to be able to come home to our own bed on one occasion, and to see the sign erected over it: 'God's in charge – not men, nor the devil!' This notice may have had a sobering effect upon the doctors who visited me there, but its impact was not lost upon me either. I was being reminded that I was not a pawn in this game of recovery, but a blood-bought, anointed servant of God whose life and future ministry is in his hands. We need to know this!

2

Things that Help

Holding on to hope

'Oh, this regime is hopeless!' That's how I felt about the 'nil-by-mouth' regime in 2005 after only a few days. This was especially so once I was discharged from hospital and had to return home laden with a tube into my small bowel and a machine for dripping in the stuff that was supposed to keep me alive. After only a very short time at home, less than a week, I was seriously dehydrated, going into another weary round of ascending cholangitis, and readmitted to hospital as an emergency. It really felt like it might be hopeless.

In our island home on Guernsey lies what was, in its day, the largest underground concrete structure in Europe. Thousands of tourists visit it every year, and shudder at the dank, threatening atmosphere. The German Underground Hospital is a lasting reminder of the crass futility of war. Built by slave labour during the German occupation of the Channel Islands, it was designed to offer a bomb-proof medical facility for *Werhmacht* troops from all over occupied Europe. In the event, it was not completed until late in 1943, and so was not pressed into service until the early part of the following year. After the D-Day landings in June of 1944, the Channel Islands began to receive Axis casualties from the front in nearby Normandy. For the first time, the vast underground structure went into action.

From day one, the huge hospital was a complete disaster. Although the facility was equipped with the very latest in X-ray and operating room technology for those times, scores of inmates died for no apparent reason. They simply gave up hope. There was something about that place that militated against all the very fine work that the doctors were doing. Cut off from all natural daylight, and built by a totalitarian occupying force, the underground hospital just didn't work. It was literally hopeless.

Hope is one of the three 'eternal virtues' of 1 Corinthians 13:13: 'Now these three remain: faith, hope and love. But the greatest of these is love.' Yet, sadly, hope is often the ugly sister of this little trinity, neglected and living in the shadow of its more famous sisters, faith and love. We generally teach that love will last for ever, outliving even prophesies and ecstatic utterances. But hope is an abiding virtue too. It may be that our estimation of the value of hope is coloured by our understanding of the word and its usage today, which is very different from the New Testament use of the word. One dictionary says hope is 'That which is desired or wished for.' This is all very well, but is far less than the Bible's use of the word implies. The old English use of the term is closer: 'To trust, expect or believe.'

I would like to go further and venture a Christian definition of the word hope: *'The confident assurance that God is good and that everything he does in my life will work out for good.'* Of course, my definition of 'good' may not be the same as God's, but it is his stated desire to work all our circumstances together for that purpose (Rom. 8:28 again). Biblical hope is not dependent upon other people, our possessions or our circumstances. It is the application of faith in the character of God and his promises, and it leads to a confident expectation of his will being done in our lives.

Fundamentally, hope is trust in the character of God. 'Put your hope in God' (Ps. 42:11) is a command not a suggestion. God is himself good – all the time. He never changes and is utterly faithful. That is why, even in the darkest night, and in the most exposed of dangers, we need to put our hope in him. Even when the writer of the book of Lamentations was gazing out at the ruins of the city of Jerusalem, he was able to affirm as a statement of hope

> Yet this I call to mind and therefore I have hope: Because of the LORD's great love we are not consumed, for his compassions never fail. They are new every morning; great is your faithfulness (Lam. 3:21–23)

If we put our hope in the unchanging character of God, we shall discover that there is no sleaze, there are no shady dealings, and there is no trace of corruption in him. There are no hidden agendas, and unlike so many earthly fathers and guardians, there is not one trace of abusive intent. God is faithful and he delights in doing us good.

> The LORD thy God in the midst of thee is mighty; he will save, he will rejoice over thee with joy; he will rest in his love, he will joy over thee with singing. (Zeph. 3:17, KJV)

Resting on a word from God

Very early on in my battle with physical pain, my wife and I found great help from the Living Bible paraphrase of 1 Peter 5:10: 'After you have suffered a little while, our God, who is full of kindness through Christ, will give you his eternal glory. He personally will come and pick you up, and set you firmly in place, and make you stronger than ever.' We both took great hope and courage from these words, especially the second part of the verse. We have kept on trusting and hoping in the promise that one day, after I had suffered a while, God would lift me up and make me 'stronger than ever'.

I know that the context of this verse is true of eternity, and will find its perfect fulfilment in heaven, but the Holy Spirit 'quickened' this scripture to my wife and I in such a way as to cause us to have hope for the here and now. That promise really sustained us, and continues to do so.

In John 4, a certain royal official came to see Jesus. His son lay sick at home in Capernaum. He begged Jesus to come and heal the son who was close to death. Jesus told him, 'You may go. Your son will live' (v. 50). This was not what the man wanted or expected. He had asked Jesus to come down to his home to heal the boy. Now he was faced with a stark choice. He had a night's journey in front of him in order to walk home. He either had to believe the word of the Lord, and go home as instructed, or else he could abandon all hope of a miracle, as it was quite clear that Jesus was not coming with him. In the event, he did the right thing and chose the first option. He held on to the word Jesus had given him regarding his son, even though he had no evidence for believing that there had been any improvement in the situation.

What a long night that must have been! There would have been times when he would have wondered if he had done the right thing by leaving Cana without the healer and miracle-worker by his side. But still, hadn't the Lord said 'Your son will live'? So, he held on to the word.

The very next day as he was walking along, his servants met him with news that the boy was living. When he asked about the time his son got better, they said to him, 'the fever left him yesterday at the seventh hour' and he realised that this was the exact time at which Jesus had said to him, 'Your son will live.'

So the man had gone his way all night long with nothing more than a promise from the Lord and a hunch that he should believe. This is sometimes what Christians are still called to do today. As in the case of the royal official in John 4, we often 'seek a word' from the Lord concerning a loved one who is in trouble, or when we are in pain ourselves. Maybe we spend time in preparation for visiting someone in need, asking God to give us a word for the situation. When we receive such a word, and the promise of God is quickened to our hearts by his Spirit, it can sustain us and others through many a long night, giving us very real hope indeed.

Understanding that pain is not pointless

The agony of acute haemorrhaging pancreatitis, the gnawing pain of chronic pancreatitis, and the sharp, breathtaking cramp of biliary colic have been my constant companions on this journey of pain.

Post-operative pain, together with – for my family and friends – the mental and emotional exhaustion of watching a loved one suffer, have been unwanted bedfellows through a score of hospital admissions and stays. Morphine and fentanyl, codeine and pethidine have just been some of the ways I have sought relief. It's hard to preach when you are on morphine. It's even harder to be in the Intensive Care Unit suffering the delusions and horrors of a bad trip on the medical form of heroin. So, what's the point of pain?

A bit like finding the reason for the existence of wasps and mosquitoes it can be hard to discern a purpose behind the creation of pain, as it causes us so much unhappiness. Yet, pain serves us in ways that we don't always fully appreciate. Pain serves us as a warning bell of something that needs to be fixed.

The whole point of physical exercise, so we are told, is to stretch the body beyond its normal limits so that it grows and develops in ways not previously possible. No pain, no gain. Apparently muscles get stronger by being pushed further than their pain barrier. When they recover, the increased blood flow and tissue activity actually leads to stronger muscles. Without the pain of being pushed, there would be no gain of growth and strengthening.

The fact is God sometimes allows pain in our lives in order to gain our attention. Now don't get me wrong here – I really wish there was another way! Yet when I read the Bible I discover that this has always been the case. Joseph found God's will for his life during his years in prison. Daniel proved God's love in a den of lions. Even the apostle Paul was thinking of this when he coined the well-known phrase 'when I am weak, then I am strong' (2 Cor. 12:10b).

On the scale of pain of various kinds, the pain of bereavement is possibly one of the worst known to man. It's not a physical pain, though it can sometimes feel so, yet it is very real. The phrase 'better to have loved and lost than never to have loved at all' can seem very stark, even unkind when one is suffering the pain of grief. Yet it reflects an aspect of human pain that is sometimes overlooked. Pain is part of the price of loving and of being loved. Nowhere is that fact more starkly and powerfully portrayed than in Mel Gibson's film *The Passion of the Christ*. The very fact that the cruel death of Jesus is called his 'passion' gives a clue to this mysterious truth – that there is a price to pay for true love. God loved his world – our world – so much that unbelievable pain was a price he thought worth paying. He gave his one and only Son so that whoever believes in him should not die eternally, but should live for ever.

Is it possible then, that some pain could actually be a gift from a loving God? 'Yet it was the LORD's will to crush him and cause him to suffer' (Is. 53:10). Not that we should look for pain in some masochistic kind of way, but rather, recognise that being in pain does not mean that God has forsaken us. Far from disqualifying us from the attention of the Lord, pain qualifies us for his loving care and support.

It's hard to see at the time, of course, but remembering that *nothing* that happens to us is pointless can remove the sense of hopelessness we feel when we are long-term sufferers, and give us strong hope even in the middle of our pain.

A different perspective

Pruning

In John 15, Jesus said that his Father is a gardener or 'vinedresser' (NASB) who prunes and cuts back the fruitful branches – not the unfruitful ones – in order that they might give even more fruit. Cutting and loss can be the prelude to great fruitfulness in God's service. This has been such a source of encouragement to me in a season where everything fruitful and good seemed to have been pared away from my life.

My father was a 'vinedresser' too. Only these vines were tomato plants, by the tens of thousands. Large greenhouses filled much of the island of Guernsey when I was a child, and my dad spent most of the spring and early summer each year leafing and trimming. The leafing was to prevent the tomato plant from spending itself and its resources too generously on the display of leaves and not enough on the forming of fruit. My job was to sweep up the leaves into piles and wheelbarrow them to the tip. The trimming was even more radical. Out of many different branches of the plant little shoots would grow that if allowed to develop, would bear fruit. If too many were allowed to grow, the fruit would be small and useless. Removing a certain number of these potential tomato-bearing shoots was essential to ultimately harvesting an acceptable crop.

In the kingdom of God, pruning is also a painful but necessary preparation for effective service. It means the loss of something good in itself, or good in its time, in order that God's best may be brought out at the right time. In order to survive this pruning process, Jesus advises us to abide in the vine – in him. This means that we must make a daily choice to go his way and rest in his love.

The purpose of pruning is to remove those things that hinder fruitfulness and develop even better fruit in us. The process is always hard, but whilst we are going through it we should try to remember that

- *Only fruitful branches get pruned.* There is no shame in pruning when the work is being done by a wise grower who knows what he's about. We should not be embarrassed about the loss or change we may have to undergo in order to let God have his way. It may even be something of a compliment that we are being subjected to this loss or trimming in our lives – God sees that we are already fruitful and wants to make us more so.

- *Pruning leads on to greater fruitfulness.* What is removed may be good but it is hindering the best. The final crop will be so much more praiseworthy to God and glorifying to him than any premature, less than fully formed product would be, however impressed we might be with it ourselves! There is a human tendency to harvest crops before they are fully ripe. As a child, I always wanted to pick the tomatoes long before my dad knew the crop was ready. I couldn't understand why he would waste apparently useful fruit-bearing shoots. But he knew what he was doing, and had his eyes on even greater goals.

- *God disciplines us because he loves us.* This is the message of Hebrews 12:5,6. 'My son, do not make light of the Lord's discipline, and do not lose heart when he rebukes you, because the Lord disciplines those he loves, and he punishes everyone he accepts as a son.' It's hard to believe that we are loved when things go wrong, but if we are being pruned or disciplined, it is because God is dealing with us as sons, not as strangers.

Just as we can begin to see our period of suffering in the light of what we understand about pruning, we can also gain a different perspective when we contemplate other issues too. And that can give us strength.

Recognising real success

When I was told that after so many hospital admissions, and so much surgery it would be necessary for me to bear a further period of illness and inactivity during the medically required fast – and to then go through even more major surgery – it was almost unbearable news. This particular bout of illness had already required time off work for a year and a half, and it was excruciating to me to have to accept yet another spell of rest. I have always been used to being so busy in Christian work, and Diane and I both really love what God has called us to do. Guilt was an added weight to bear in all this, because I felt that as God's servant I was in some way failing him by remaining sick and being out of frontline ministry. All this got me thinking about what real success in life or ministry might look like.

God does not measure success in the same way that we usually presume. Is God looking for super-saints? Does he always seek mega-churches? Does he want us to be fit and productive in all circumstances, or is it possible that he's after something deeper, something more?

I wonder, do you see God as an executive workaholic who expects his servants to be the same? I did. That pattern of thinking was formed early in my ministry. I believed that successful ministries meant getting up early to pray and seek God long before breakfast, labouring in the study or the office all morning, visiting people in their own homes all afternoon, dashing home for tea, and then running off to long evening meetings… and all this with never a day off! My mentors in the ministry seemed to embody this lifestyle. They led growing churches with dynamic ministries that often took them overseas. Now, it may have been right for them to do all of that (only they and their families will know the answer to that) but it seems that it is not the particular road that my heavenly Father has called *me* to walk upon.

When you think about it, Jesus turned all the rules of success upside down. He trained for thirty years in order to minister for three instead of the other way around as it is in most modern ministry. He never wrote an article or a book, or even attended college. He had no PA, no secretary and no diary as far as we know, and never used more than a donkey as a vehicle in his travels. His ministry was dogged by confrontation and betrayal, attack and vilification. His staff failed him, his family thought he was crazy, and he spent so much time praying in remote places that his team had to send out search parties to find him on occasions. Finally, of course, he was condemned by the highest court in the land and executed like a common criminal. Yet this ministry was a success. It fulfilled the Father's plan for it, formed before the world began. Whilst most other leaders of that era are forgotten or dimly known, Jesus is worshipped by countless millions around the world today.

So what was the secret of his success? There were several, but one of them was being content to discover the Father's will and do it with joy. Jesus did that which he saw the Father doing. He delighted in the works prepared for him to do.

Early on in my trials I read this wonderful verse from the Living Bible, 'let us run with patience the particular race that God has set before us' (Heb. 12:1b). It really helps to know that God has a particular race that he has set out for *me* to run. It is special just for *me*. We must not get distracted by looking at others who are running a different race, if that is the particular race God has called them to run. Success for me is to run the race that God has chosen for me, and to finish it well. Running a race is not much use if you don't finish well. Too many of us start and fail to finish. Yet, it really matters how we finish. Success can only really be known in retrospect.

Another aspect of success that may not be fully appreciated is in the arena of our relationships, and especially with our children. Too many famous and much travelled celebrities have left a trail of broken hearts behind them on their journey through their kind of successes. As it has often been said, nobody ever lies on their deathbed and says, 'I wish I'd spent more time at the office!'

So, here's a different perspective again; perhaps I should take the pressure off myself and leave matters of success and failure for God to resolve in eternity. Meanwhile, if I run with perseverance the particular race he has called me to pursue, even if it is the road marked with suffering, I surely won't go far wrong.

Joyful acceptance

One of the tactics with which you learn to cope with the indignities and humiliations of being a hospital patient over a long period is to become resigned to your lot. Resignation is just kind of accepting whatever comes along – another blood test, another tube, yet another scan, and so on. If you think too much about it you might not be able to face it, so you just 'lie back and think of England'! Resignation, the blind, unquestioning surrender to what is happening to you is also apparently one of the techniques for enduring torture. By reckoning themselves as good as dead, and trying not to think through the consequences of their situation, or even to imagine the hope of release or rescue, torture victims can stand up to the most horrendous assaults on their persons. I suppose there is an element of Christian teaching in this in that we are told to 'reckon ourselves dead' and that we are 'crucified in Christ'.

However, resignation is not what the Bible means by embracing the will of God. Just doing the will of God reluctantly, through gritted teeth, is to invite problems in our walk with our Lord. No. What God is calling us to do is to embrace his will for us – with joy. Yes, joy!

Doing God's will with joy really is the only way to do it. Any kind of reluctance, or a 'grin and bear it' attitude will rob us of the peace and assurance that come from delighting in his will. In Philippians 2, Paul urged his readers to have the same attitude as Jesus; part of that attitude was the desire to do everything the Father asked. 'Therefore, when Christ came into the world, he said: ... "I have come to do your will, O God"' (Heb. 10:5,7b).

When the Son of God left heaven, he was not submitting to his Father's plan in any kind of grudging way, but rather delighting in it. It's amazing that even though he knew he was facing the cross, Jesus was able to delight to do the Father's will. The apostle Paul, like Jesus, had a great desire to please God. 'So we make it our goal to please him, whether we are at home in the body or away from it' (2 Cor. 5:9).

Joy in trials and embracing God's way must be much more than a reluctant surrender. It must be a joyful acceptance that God knows best, that he loves us perfectly, and that we choose to trust that loving care to see us through.

I realise that some of you will be shaking your heads at this point. Joyful acceptance of pain and suffering just doesn't seem realistic... or possible. But look to Jesus. If you really can't feel joy in your situation – and frankly, it's not something you can 'work up' – then don't despair. Ask Jesus to give *his* joy to you. The perspective of joyful acceptance really can help in the darkest of times.

Learning contentment

Much in the same way as joyful acceptance comes contentment. Jesus was content to do his Father's will. Likewise, it appears that despite all his troubles, the apostle Paul had learned the secret of contentment: 'I have learned the secret of being content in any and every situation' (Phil. 4:12). Now 'contentment' is not an easy thing to feel, especially when you are in pain or passing through tough times. But maybe part of the problem is a misunderstanding of what biblical contentment really is, and what it is not.

Contentment for the Christian is not the same as complacency. Paul was not complacent even though he had learned the secret of being content. He agonised, for instance, over the eternal destiny of his beloved people the Jews (see Rom. 9:1–5). He also longed for the Christians in Galatia to mature in Christ, to the point of feeling physical pain on their behalf (see Gal. 4:19). Yet despite these strong passions, Paul does not seem to have been a driven man. The evidence of Philippians 4 is that he knew an underlying peace and security in all circumstances.

Being content did not stop Paul longing for more of God either, or stretching for more in the kingdom of God. Contentment is not the same as just coasting along on the strength of past experiences alone. In Philippians 3:12–14, Paul shows that his desire to press forward and become mature in Christ was an all consuming passion, despite his underlying contentment. Nor was this contentment a form of pride or conceit, for which it could so easily have been mistaken. It appears from 1 Timothy 1:15 that the contented Paul still thought of himself as the chief of sinners, and knew that all he possessed was his by the grace of God through Christ.

He mourned his sin and wanted to do better, but he had still discovered the foundation of inner peace that contentment provides.

So what does contentment mean for the Christian believer? Well, in the passage mentioned above in Philippians 4, the context is all about money. Basically, Paul was saying that whether 'well fed or hungry' he had learned to be content in God. Paul was at ease. He did not presume that God had abandoned him if things got tough. Whenever the word 'content' appears in Scripture it is usually to do with money. If you want to see this, look at 1 Timothy 6:6–10, and Hebrews 13:5: 'Keep your lives free from the love of money and be content with what you have, because God has said, "Never will I leave you; never will I forsake you."' Now, that is not easy when you are on sickness or invalidity benefits and facing an unknown future. Yet, if we belong to Christ, and he is Lord of our lives, *the onus for the provision of our daily needs is upon his shoulders.* God has promised to be our provider in all circumstances. Even when the breadwinner is affected by pain and illness, that promise stands.

Biblical contentment also leads to freedom from the fear of death and the future. This is clearly seen in the testimony of the Chinese Christian leader, Brother Yun, whose book *The Heavenly Man*[7] has exposed to millions the courage and bravery of ordinary believers who are suffering for their faith, yet have great peace in their hearts.

Biblical contentment also seems to set people free from the stress of always having to please others. This can be a terrible burden to bear when we are already in pain from other causes. Ultimately, while we don't want to offend others, we are the Lord's servants now, and we live to please him. 'If we live, we live to the

Lord; and if we die, we die to the Lord. So, whether we live or die, we belong to the Lord' (Rom. 14:8).

So how do we get this contentment – what is the secret of being content in all circumstances? Well, contentment is something we learn through the harder experiences of life. In Philippians 4 there are some keys.

- *A personal relationship with Jesus Christ.* Verse 13 says: 'I can do everything through him who gives me strength.' It's the daily walk with Christ that matters. For instance, people like Brother Yun who may be in prison for their faith cannot meet with believers, yet the fellowship of the Lord's sufferings means that Jesus is constantly with them, sympathising with them in their trials, and giving them supernatural strength to endure.
- *Rejoicing in the Lord in all circumstances.* Verse 4 says: 'Rejoice in the Lord always. I will say it again: Rejoice!' This again is an important key to enduring difficult or even discouraging circumstances. Paul had proved this quite literally when he and Silas were thrown into prison following a sound thrashing in Philippi, the very town to which he later addressed his letter. In Acts 16 we read that despite their wounds and circumstances, at about midnight Paul and Silas were praying and singing hymns to God! Suddenly there was such a violent earthquake that the foundations of the prison were shaken. The prison doors flew open, and everybody's chains came loose. It appears that the miraculous intervention followed on from their praising, but even if it had not, these early Christian were not prepared to abandon their hope in God. (Quite a good example of the joyful acceptance we were reading about earlier!)

- *Praying about everything.* Verse 6 says: 'Do not be anxious about anything, but in everything, by prayer and petition, with thanksgiving, present your requests to God.' This is another antidote to anxiety. Praying about everything means exactly that. God is big enough to take our strongest crying and complaint in prayer. The majority of the psalms were laments – complaints which were being poured out before the Lord in prayer.

If you struggle to know contentment in your situation, again, you're not alone. Bring it to the One who loves you best, and ask for his help.

Hanging on to eternity

'He has ... set eternity in the hearts of men; yet they cannot fathom what God has done from beginning to end' (Ecc. 3:11b). The reality of eternal life is something that should help us to keep hanging in there through the storms of life, yet is so difficult to grasp. Perhaps because life on earth is so comfortable for many in the West, it has become more difficult for us to picture the vivid reality of the world that awaits us beyond this one. However, heaven is real, and the Lord is preparing a place for us there. If we can hold on to that promise, it will set our trials into their proper, temporary perspective.

I have recently been watching a DVD reconstruction of the case of a man called Ian McCormack whose godless lifestyle of surfing, drugs and drink was brought to a sudden halt by an encounter with death.[8] He was diving off the coast of Mauritius when he was stung by a deadly jellyfish. His near-death experience took place in a hospital where he succumbed to the vicious poison that had been left in his system. During his journey to that hospital in an ambulance, he had tried to pray the only prayer he could remember from his youth, the Lord's Prayer. As he did so, his spiritual eyes were opened to understand its true meaning for the first time in his adult life. When his heart stopped beating in the hospital, he first felt surrounded by the most intense and menacing darkness which was suddenly shattered by the presence of a powerful light. The light and a sense of great love drew him up into a doorway from which he viewed a fabulous world of rolling hills, pastureland and mountains. He was given the chance to go back, and for the sake of his mother (whom he realised would have prayed for him to become a Christian and would never know that he had done so), he was willing to return. The result is a man with a powerful ministry, winning many to the Christian faith. Yes, *heaven is real.*

If we can get hold of this truth it will comfort and encourage us: 'Now we know that if the earthly tent we live in is destroyed, we have a building from God, an eternal house in heaven, not built by human hands. Meanwhile we groan, longing to be clothed with our heavenly dwelling' (2 Cor. 5:1).

Both the Bible verses we have quoted, however, also include a healthy dose of reality. The first, from Ecclesiastes, says that although God has set eternity in our hearts we still cannot fathom what God is doing in the here and now. The second teaches that despite the wonderful assurance that there is a lasting building for us in heaven when we are done with our earthly tent, we still groan, longing to be there! The limited earthly perspective that most of us have means that confusion about God's purposes (and groaning in the meantime) are inevitable parts of our sufferings.

We can help ourselves to overcome these very human hindrances by choosing to remind ourselves often that our eternal home – our real home – is in heaven. Diane and I have lived in some beautiful places. We had two wonderful years in the Seychelles on a mountainside overlooking the town of Victoria, and then our years in Zimbabwe surrounded by mountains. In Guernsey we lived on a headland with the sea on three sides of us and common land to walk on. When we are marvelling at the stunning beauty of God's creation, we remind each other that heaven is even better than this.

Spend time reading the last chapters of Revelation; remember that heaven is our *real* home. Encourage yourself with this, the ultimate different perspective.

The power of forgiveness

During the long period of abstinence that preceded the latest round of major surgery, there was a lot of extra time available to think about the deeper things of life. One of those surrounded the whole area of forgiveness, and my need to let go of those who had hurt me during my illness in various ways. I even had to deal with how I was feeling about one particular doctor on the surgical team whose attitude seemed appalling and caused us such unnecessary hurt and upset.

In Matthew 18:21–35, Jesus responds to a searching question from Peter in which he asks, with a hint of magnanimity in his voice, 'Lord, how much forgiveness do I owe others? How often must I go on forgiving?' Jesus gave the answer in story form that was so powerful it was shocking. He told about a king who wanted to settle accounts with his servants. As he began the settlement, a man came before him who owed him a huge amount of money. Obviously unable to pay such a ridiculously large amount, the king ordered that he and his wife and his children and all that he had be sold to repay the debt. When, however, the servant begged for time, his master took pity on him, cancelled the debt and let him go.

Amazingly, and in stark contrast, that forgiven servant went out, found one of his fellow servants who owed him a fairly small sum, grabbed him and demanded payment. The poor man's choking plea for mercy was refused. He was thrown into prison until he could pay the debt. When this came to the ears of the king he was enraged.

The moral of the tale is fairly clear. Christians have been forgiven a debt so great that they could never have hoped to repay it themselves. The King's own son paid the debt for us at Calvary. That means that we owe one another a great debt of forgiveness. Sadly it is not often forthcoming, and the resultant bitterness and suppressed rage (which can express itself in depression and even self-harm) causes more damage to the one refusing to forgive than to the one who needs the forgiveness.

Satan (a prosecuting counsel – see Zech. 3) enjoys using justice for his own ends. When we receive the grace of God through Christ, and then give it to others, Satan is unemployed. When we refuse to forgive and hold on to bitterness and resentment, we join Satan in his work.

What is forgiveness? Here's a definition to think about. It is to treat the one who sinned as if they had not. And to choose never to remember the sin again. As we remember how much God has forgiven us, then we will forgive others. But it's hard, isn't it? Forgiveness is not natural. No; it is *supernatural*. Forgiveness is God's work and we need his help to be able to do it. Even if you forgive and fail, forgive and fail, you are still a forgiver. There are, however, quite serious consequences that arise out of an unwillingness to forgive. When we refuse to forgive

- *We block the flow of forgiveness in our own lives.* 'For if you forgive men when they sin against you, your heavenly Father will also forgive you. But if you do not forgive men their sins, your Father will not forgive your sins' (Mt. 6:14). Sometimes we need to forgive ourselves, based on the facts of what Christ has done for us, not based upon our feelings. Refusing to forgive others (or ourselves when God says we are forgiven) is like erecting a dam in a stream. It stops the flow of forgiveness in our lives.

- *We are no longer a witness for the forgiving King.* In the story we have just thought about, the other servants saw what was happening and they said, 'This is inconsistent... this man is a hypocrite!' The forgiven servant lost all his credibility in the eyes of others because of his unforgiving attitude. Those of us who refuse to forgive live in danger of forfeiting the respect of those whom we seek to influence for the kingdom of God. There is nothing more ugly and repulsive to non-Christians than to see believers who hate one another or who refuse to forgive. It is so often the thing that is quoted by people as an excuse for not going to church any longer.

- *We lose our spiritual authority.* Our prayers lose their effectiveness and become hollow and empty (see Mk. 11:24,25). This is particularly the case when the problem is between husbands and wives, as we see in 1 Peter 3:7. But there are many blessings to be had from forgiving those who offended us. The medical profession is also coming to realise the power of forgiveness.

What are some of the benefits of forgiveness? Forgiveness can set us free from the awful load of having to keep certain things secret. Issues can be dealt with that otherwise might continue to fester and cause harm. Forgiveness can also set us free from bitterness. Few sins are as devastating to the sinner as bitterness. It poisons the person who is bitter and defiles all that they come into contact with (see Heb. 12:15). Forgiveness also has the power to defuse hatred and the destruction that it can cause.[9]

It has been well said that unforgiveness does not actually damage the one who hurt us; it damages the one who does not forgive. It is interesting to contemplate the power of forgiveness in relation to health and healing... isn't it?

Letting go

Someone once told me that the pathway to peace is learning to 'let go' of people or of situations that really trouble us. But to let go of someone you love and put them into the hands of God can be one of the hardest things I think we can ever do.

To let go of someone doesn't mean we stop caring about them. Instead, we choose to believe that God can accomplish what we can't. We place our trust in God – his will, not ours, be done; we focus on him alone. But to 'let go and let God' is not easy!

Letting go is not just something we have to do in prayer for others. I learned that when it became a big part of what God was doing with me throughout my illness, and especially during the fast and surgery. I was being called (more pressed really) to pray every day what can only be called 'the prayer of relinquishment'. By that I mean being willing to let go of anything, however good and precious, in order that God's will would be done, that he might accomplish all that he has planned for us. In my case the prayer of relinquishment meant letting go of the preaching ministry. It meant being silent for over a year. It also required me to let go of the church and pastorate that I really loved at Shiloh, where both Diane and I felt that there was so much potential for future fruitfulness. Time and again I found myself being challenged by the Holy Spirit to pray that prayer and let it all go.

In Genesis 22 we have the ultimate illustration of this letting go. Abraham had waited many years for the answer to his prayers and the fulfilment of God's promises. The birth of Isaac – when his wife was long past the age of childbearing – was all that the couple could have dreamed, and more. For the first time in years they felt excited about the future. Their hopes were all pinned on this one young boy. Then suddenly God spoke to Abraham in ways that must have seemed incredible. He told him to sacrifice the boy as a burnt offering. Such a command must have seemed scandalous. Child sacrifice was the way of the heathen, not the way of those who walk with the one true God! And how could God's promises be fulfilled if Abraham sacrificed his precious son? Yet the book of Hebrews shows us that Abraham obeyed because he believed that if he did, then the Lord would fulfil his own word, even if it meant bringing the dead back to life again. Now *that's* faith!

The strange thing about letting go is that often it is only when you do it that you receive the thing you let go back again. That's what happened to Abraham after he and Isaac had suffered the agony of the long walk to Mount Moriah and the act of placing the boy upon the altar. When the old man finally let go, God provided a ram to take Isaac's place. Only in the surrender of relinquishment would Abraham be in the right place at the right moment to be able to make use of God's provided sacrifice. That is how it is for us too. So let go. And be encouraged.

Becoming real

Margery Williams' classic tale of *The Velveteen Rabbit*[10] is the story of a toy rabbit that started out all lovely and new but, as a Christmas present to a boy who absolutely adored him, began to get shabbier and shabbier purely because he was being *loved*. After talking to another toy he realised that it is when you are loved that you become 'real'... although others might see you as shabby and broken. And becoming real takes time.

Near our island home, on the headland where we walk our dog, is a large rock on which some graffiti artist has been at work. They have painted the phrase 'La la Land' on the rock, and every time Diane and I walk past it we usually say to each other, 'Here we go into La la Land again!' Sadly, evangelical Christians are not best known for their ability to be 'real'. In fact, in our experience, a lot of us live in 'la la land' – a place somewhere between church and cloud-cuckoo-land! In 'La la Land' prayers are always answered just as you pray them, especially if you have sufficient faith, or are living the 'victorious Christian life'. 'La la Land' knows no negativity, being afraid – being *very* afraid – of putting anything negative into words in case it becomes a fact just because you said it! (Inhabitants of 'La la Land' have noticed that in the Genesis 1 record of creation, God said certain things and they were thus created, and the inference is taken that if they are not careful, anything they say may also become part of their altered reality.) But what happens when people hear testimonies of success without the flip-side of failure? They become discouraged! They think that those of us who *aren't real* about the whole story don't struggle – while they do. We must be real. Remember the great failures of Scripture? David committed adultery and murder before he found forgiveness and restoration. We are not plaster saints. We are flesh and blood, human beings. We get it wrong. We fail. But we are saved by God's free, unmerited favour – his grace, his love. And *that's* the message of hope we can share with others in and through our pain.

Having said that, I am not knocking the need to speak out positive, good things and use encouraging and helpful words as opposed to dwelling on the negative. The teaching of Ephesians 4:29 – 'Do not let any unwholesome talk come out of your mouths, but only what is helpful for building others up according to their needs, that it may benefit those who listen' – is important for the well-being of Christians and Christian communities. Yet Ephesians 4:15 says we should speak the truth in love! Surely a sign of real relationship is that you can be real with people and not forfeit their love or care. Holding back from telling trusted individuals how it really is because of a fear that speaking out the very words will make things worse is akin to a medieval type of superstition about the power of curses.

When we are tempted to jump on to the attractive bandwagon of 'what you say is what you get' and that strange idea that if you deny reality you are living on some higher plane of faith, we need to look at the Bible. The book of Psalms, for instance is full of lament, sorrow, pain and unanswered prayer.

I say to God my Rock, 'Why have you forgotten me? Why must I go about mourning, oppressed by the enemy?' My bones suffer mortal agony as my foes taunt me, saying to me all day long, 'Where is your God?' Why are you downcast, O my soul? Why so disturbed within me? (Ps. 42:9–11a)

Obviously no fear of creating some kind of negative reality there! Some of the Old Testament prophets were just as honest in their prayers, like Jeremiah who cursed the very day that he had been born, and Habakkuk who felt that God was just not listening to him. Isn't it wonderful to read his closing verses?

Though the fig-tree does not bud and there are no grapes on the vines, though the olive crop fails and the fields produce no food, though there are no sheep in the pen and no cattle in the stalls, yet I will rejoice in the LORD, I will be joyful in God my Saviour (Hab. 3:17–18)

It seems that Habakkuk had come to understand that God has a purpose in those barren times as well as the good. What is important though is that the prophet does not do any 'positive confessing' that things are anything other than what they clearly are – barren. He doesn't confess that fig trees are about to burst into fruit, or that there must be sheep in the pen 'by faith'. No, he just gets real and decides that in face of an awful reality on the ground, God is greater than that reality and still deserves his praise. That's faith – the faith that goes through disappointment into trusting God when it appears that all is lost.

I have really had to settle it in my mind that I would be utterly real with people during my period of need. It can be very hard in Christian leadership, when you realise that your words and actions can affect others, and the news you have is not what you would like it to be. Yet, there can be no blessing on a lie. The Holy Spirit is the spirit of truth and can only bless truth, not denial, exaggeration or evasion. So, Diane and I both decided to get real and stay real. Let's think about some of the benefits of getting real with each other:

- *We would avoid platitudes,* such as 'Well, keep trusting dear!' or 'God is still on the throne!' instead of the reality that weeps with those who weep and says things like 'I'm so sorry you feel that way today and I want you to know that I'm here for you.'
- *We would avoid wasting so much time.* Isn't it a pity that by the time many of us 'get real' we are broken and shabby? If only we could learn the delights of reality much earlier in life and build friendships and love that are based on how things really are and not on how we want them to be, or how we want them to appear!
- *We would avoid a false representation of God.* Jesus is described in John 14:6 as 'the way and the truth and the life'. He's the truth, not the grand pretence. If we avoid reality because it is messy and unpalatable we run the danger of making people think that our God is living in 'La, la Land' and can't cope with reality. This is far from the truth and a parody of who he is. Be real! God can take it. Jesus cried from the cross 'My God, my God, why have you forsaken me?' And in 1 Peter 5:7, we are urged to 'Cast all your anxiety on him because he cares for you.'
- *We would avoid unhealthy denial.* I have spent a lot of the last decade in denial about my pain. I didn't want to own it or its consequences for my ministry. So I chose to pretend that it wasn't there, and to say as much if anyone asked. Finally Diane could stand my

denial no longer and spoke to a trusted elder to tell him about the amount of morphine I was taking just to get me through the day, and the agony in which I was returning home after services. Reality led to understanding, and space was created for me to find help and get some relief, however long it took.

- *We would avoid isolation.* A pastor's wife had suffered from depression for several years, but had done her level best not to let it show. Her attempts at keeping up appearances were commendable but painful to her and her husband. Finally, one day, sitting in church, her reserve broke and she began to sob during a service. She thought the end had come, that her credibility as a pastor's wife and Christian leader had just disappeared out of the window, but what happened that day was to amaze her. Within a very short time she was surrounded by three really caring ladies from the congregation. They pledged to love her and be there for her for as long as it took for her to recover. They were practical, persistent, loving, prayerful and wise. Together they won the war over depression. That day was not the end, but the beginning.

The beginning of reality and reality breaks down walls of isolation and fear. I urge you, be real with God – and with others.

Perseverance

In all of this, we need to persevere. Sometimes 'hanging in there' means precisely that – just hanging on hoping for better days. Perseverance is one of the works of the Holy Spirit in us, and can be strengthened by the daily choices we make. The Greek word for perseverance literally means 'the ability to handle pressure'. It has its place in our lives as part of the reason why God allows suffering in the first place – to produce perseverance (see Rom. 5:3).

I suppose that Diane and I learned the value of perseverance when we were missionaries in Zimbabwe. We watched the African families coping with loss, grief and poverty; their ability to keep praising God when literally all was being stripped from them was awe-inspiring. The fact that they could walk thirty or forty kilometres to attend convention meetings in the baking heat after long weeks spent at work was testimony to their gift of endurance. They would stand uncomplainingly in long hot queues for hours on end just to be able to buy a bag of sugar or a sack of maize-meal – and seemed to enjoy the opportunity for a good chat!

I have never been very good at anything that demands stamina. My attempts at swimming pool lengths are pretty derisory, and family walks are more like strolls. Whenever I had to drive any distance in Africa – and long journeys were often required in my ministry there – I would stop and rest overnight in guest houses and hotels, breaking the journey whenever I could. Yet during this illness, I have had to grow new muscles in the area of my ability to persevere. Twelve times in twelve months from 2004 to 2005 I was admitted to hospital and many more times have followed since. Long periods of waiting for doctors' rounds, scanning machines, test results and so forth all take their toll. You simply have to choose not be in a hurry and to hang in there, hoping for better days. Getting irate and hot under the collar is not good for the blood pressure or for the soul. 'You need to persevere' is sometimes a calling from God, and if that is the case, then he will give us the ability so to do if we ask him.

The King James Version of the Bible calls one aspect of the fruit of the Spirit in Galatians 5:22 'longsuffering'. Now there's a term for perseverance! Most of us today want everything to be quick, instant coffee, microwave meals – ding ding! and that's it! But the kingdom of God is not like that. There are no dehydrated short cuts to maturity in the Christian life, to which you simply add the water of prayer and it's all done in seconds. No, God works like a farmer on us, patiently turning over the soil, planting the seed, tending the young plants, weeding, pruning, and waiting until a harvest of fruit is gathered. He is eternal and can therefore afford to wait. He is not in a hurry to produce the kind of good fruit that is on his agenda.

So, when tempted to cut the whole process short and run for cover, I remind myself of God's eternal perspective and ask him to help me to hang in there. The wonderful thing is all things pass; circumstances *do* change; things will not always be the same. There will come a final day of pain and an end to this battle with ill health, but until that day we are called to persevere (see Col. 1:10–12).

Conclusion

The doctor knelt at the bedside. I was glad that he had come, and comforted by his presence. What I was not prepared for was the look of pity in his eyes.

'I am so sorry, Eric. You just have no quality of life at all. I am going to have to send you into hospital again.'

I was too weak to argue. Once again I was battling with one of the several allergies which have hampered pain control and recovery in this condition. This time it was a severe and unusual allergic reaction to fentanyl,[11] administered via skin patches. After a long spell of taking morphine, my GP had suggested that it might be preferable to take opiates by skin patch instead. This was to avoid some of the side-effects that oral pain relievers can cause.

During recent discussions (sometimes quite heated ones) with Christian friends, concerning proposed changes in legislation about euthanasia, I have heard the claim made that all pain is controllable. I do not believe that to be true, except where the patient is rendered unconscious. Sometimes it is necessary for pain to be endured, to be coped with, without effective relief. At least that has been my experience after years of treating pain with opiates, sometimes as strong as the medical equivalent of heroin. Chronic extreme pain can be a very heavy burden to bear.

How do we cope when the pain we have prayed will be removed actually gets worse? I have learnt all this the hard way yet am convinced that no Christian should have to suffer pain alone. It need not be like this. There are ways to cope with pain, and to overcome it. Not all pain is curable, but it should be manageable. We don't need to be just victims of pain; we can fight back, and in many cases, overcome.

There are things that hinder and things that help. For the Christian there are issues that relate to our walk with God that will either bring us aid or hold us back. The obvious dangers of having a 'stiff upper lip', rebellion (even sweet rebellion), rejection, fear, disappointment, isolation, self-pity and unhealthy dependency can hinder any of us, however sincere, in our struggle to cope with chronic pain. Yet there are real benefits to be had by drawing on spiritual resources in our battle with our bodies. And we have seen in this section that there are attitudes too that can really help. Hope – a word from God, and knowing pain is not pointless – having a different perspective on pruning, success, and understanding joyful acceptance and contentment within our situation, focusing on the reality of eternity; knowing the power of forgiveness, letting go, choosing to be real, and finally, perseverance. These are real assets in our fight.

There is more to healing than the alleviation of symptoms. The reason for the very existence of the church is that it should be a fountain of life and healing, and a place of support in times of crisis and need. That belief keeps me sane, and is the basis for this present work. Yet for you too, if you are a sufferer of pain, I am writing today. You are not alone in your suffering. God knows, pain is bad enough, but the misunderstanding and isolation that it brings is an unnecessary burden that a so-called caring society lays on weary shoulders. Approached in the right way, all these effects of pain can be managed so as to be minimised in their destructive power. The One who made you *loves* you and cares too much about you to leave you where you are. If the incarnation means anything, it signifies that we are not alone in our pain.

As we have seen, coping with pain means acknowledging its reality. Denial is a technique that some have used in meditation-type methods for distraction from pain, but it is simply not intellectually acceptable for the Christian who believes in the truth. Neither the sufferer nor those caring for them should ignore or deny pain. It must be acknowledged and faced, not in some kind of self-pitying way, but in order to tackle it head-on. If loneliness is the dark side of the planet Pain, then carers need to enable their loved ones to express how they are feeling without it being belittled, mocked or ignored. And who knows best how bad the pain is? The patient! We ought not to presume that other people show their pain in the same way that we might, or that they feel it as we would. Every sufferer is an individual and their pain levels are theirs alone. So, if you want to know, ask the patient.

Coping with pain also means attacking it with every weapon in the armoury. Yes, use drugs that help you without too many side-effects, but explore other methods too, always keeping in mind the danger of getting sidetracked into methods that are occultist in origin. When I was offered acupuncture I refused it, believing it to be inconsistent with my Christian principles and suspecting that it might be a fringe-occult activity. Yet when attending a Pastors' conference I met some

Korean Pentecostal pastors who challenged my attitude by asking what right we in the West had to condemn their traditional method of pain control out of hand when our so-called conventional medicine includes the use of such drugs as opium and even heroin with their obvious mind-bending side effects and addictive dangers. Every Christian should be clear in his or her mind as to whether or not God wants them to go down this road, but onlookers who are not suffering their pain should withhold their judgement.

There are real concerns in the Christian community about many forms of alternative therapies. Principally a lot of them are based upon occult roots or involve fringe-occult activities. There is quite a lot of literature available as to the dangers of these so-called therapies and the possible side effects for believers and non-believers alike. I would just like to sound a note of caution about not judging all alternative therapies too hastily or too harshly, but to do the necessary research or consult your pastors and leaders, and then make it a matter of prayer before making your own decision as to whether to be involved or not. Coping with pain is always a very individual experience anyway. There are numerous pain-control clinics and courses, books and self-help guides, and some of them may be really wacky. Only you know what helps, and you should follow it through 'as unto the Lord' asking for his guidance and blessing. What you can be sure of is that the control of your pain is a procedure that is close to his heart as he watches his beloved child struggling day after day and night after night in agony. 'He knows – he loves – he cares.' Jesus refused the common anaesthesia of his day, vinegar like wine mixed with gall, not because he was against pain control, but because he wanted to enter into our deepest pain. When you are in yours,

hold on to his hand, and hang in there, knowing that
the One who made you suffers beside you, and will not
let you go.

Part Three

Surviving Storms

Introduction

Ever since the Bible book of Job it has been fairly obvious to the careful reader that, being a believer, and being in the service of God, is no ticket to immunity from facing life's storms. In fact, it may even seem that the opposite is the case, and that people of no faith appear to get on better than those of us who are doing our level best to please God.

In this part, we will take a fresh look at two characters that were familiar with suffering. In the shorter section, we will look at about Job. And then we will go on to the apostle Paul, as we think about the inevitability of storms in the Christian life.

1

The trials of Job

Have you ever thought about this... God chose Job for trials because he was pleased with him, not because Job had done anything wrong?

Job lost nearly everything and everybody that he held dear – his children, his wealth, his health, even the support of his wife (Job 2:9). He was also faced with the harsh criticism of his friends – Eliphaz in particular (see Job 22:21–26), who sounded so spiritual and yet was so wrong. All these relatives and friends worked life out on the basis of a simple but erroneous formula

$$\text{sin} = \text{suffering}$$
$$\text{doing good} = \text{prosperity}$$

This formula might be straightforward, but it is not correct! Job 1:6–12 shows how Satan was given permission by God to afflict Job because the Lord trusted Job with this trial.

One day the angels came to present themselves before the LORD, and Satan also came with them. The LORD said to Satan, 'Where have you come from?' Satan answered the LORD, 'From roaming through the earth and going to and fro in it.'

Then the LORD said to Satan, 'Have you considered my servant Job? There is no-one on earth like him; he is blameless and upright, a man who fears God and shuns evil.'

'Does Job fear God for nothing?' Satan replied. 'Have you not put a hedge around him and his household and everything he has? You have blessed the work of his hands, so that his flocks and herds are spread throughout the land. But stretch out your hand and strike everything he has, and he will surely curse you to your face.'

The LORD said to Satan, 'Very well, then, everything he has is in your hands, but on the man himself do not lay a finger.'

Then Satan went out from the presence of the LORD.

Far from being punished for unconfessed sin, Job was being held up by the Lord as an example of faith and trust in adversity.

By chapter 23 Job laments the fact that sometimes in trials it is so hard to sense God's presence. 'But if I go to the east, he is not there; if I go to the west, I do not find him. When he is at work in the north, I do not see him; when he turns to the south, I catch no glimpse of him. But he knows the way that I take; when he has tested me, I shall come forth as gold' (Job 23:8–10). The hardest trial of all can be the struggle to find God even when you know that he is your Redeemer (see Job 19:25). Yet Job made choices that were to see him through.

Choosing to trust

He chose to trust in God, not in himself. As we have already seen, but repeated here because it is so important: 'But he knows the way that I take; when he has tested me, I shall come forth as gold.' In other words Job was saying 'I don't know what's going on but he does, so I am going to trust that when this is through, I will be a better person for it.' This idea is repeated in the New Testament by someone else who knew a few things about suffering, James, the brother of the Lord Jesus Christ. 'You have heard of Job's perseverance and have seen what the Lord finally brought about. The Lord is full of compassion and mercy' (Jas. 5:11). Job's perseverance was built upon trust.

Real spirituality is to recognise that the circumstances of our lives, far from hindering us in our ministry and Christianity could actually be an opportunity for God to change us in ways that would not be possible without the pain and suffering that we experience during storms.

> In this you greatly rejoice, though now for a little while you may have had to suffer grief in all kinds of trials. These have come so that your faith – of greater worth than gold, which perishes even though refined by fire – may be proved genuine and may result in praise, glory and honour when Jesus Christ is revealed (1 Pet. 1:6,7).

Choosing to treasure God's Word

He chose to treasure God's Word. 'I have not departed from the commands of his lips; I have treasured the words of his mouth more than my daily bread.' Eliphaz had goaded him that if he really treasured the Word of God he would not be in the state he was in. Job countered by his simple testimony, 'I love God's words more than food' (not just the return of his prosperity). At this stage in history the Word of God was not yet written down, but it is for us. We need to be hungry for that Word whatever is going on in our lives. It is like a pack of rations in a lifeboat. I heard a sermon where the speaker remarked that Martin Luther once said that if it wasn't for tribulation, he would not have understood the Scriptures. Trouble and God's Word go together in synergistic ways that affect us more together than they ever would apart. Job's testimony is strengthened by the fact that he was also able to say that he had not departed from God's commands – so that the Bible is not only our comfort, it is our daily guide to behaviour and attitudes.

Choosing to worship

He chose to remain a worshipper. It was remarkable, but Job did not allow his own sorrow to rob him of his intimacy with God. Right from the start of his trials he made a decision to worship even when he did not feel like it (see Job 1:20,21). Some Christians struggle to worship when all is going well, let alone when trials and trouble come. In Job's worship, he did not charge God with wrongdoing. He would be real before God, but not accusatory. Worship helps us to focus on the goodness and faithfulness of God rather than our needs.

Choosing to pray

He chose to pray for others. Even for those who had accused and abused him (see Job 42:8,9). God accepted Job's prayer because of the cost that was involved. These men had mocked and berated him, but Job was still willing to pray for them. The net result of all this was that Job's end was greater than his beginning. He was blessed in his family and his business as a result of pleasing God in the midst of storms rather than pleasing self.

A last word

As I mentioned earlier, I am impressed that Job could see the overruling hand of God in his circumstances. He says: 'But now [God] has taken away my strength. You [O Lord] have made desolate all my family and associates. You have laid firm hold on me and have shrivelled me up...and my leanness [and wretched state of body]...testify to my face' (Job 16:7,8, Amplified Version). Knowing God was at work with me helped me very much when I was going through one of my most desolate times. I hope it is something for you to reflect upon too.

2

Paul's life-threatening storm

Some time ago we flew to the UK from Guernsey aboard a medium-sized turboprop airliner during a hurricane. Why we did so I'm still not sure, because we knew throughout the day preceding our flight that the howling gale-force winds were increasing in intensity. Our son, Matthew, warned us several times that he had heard the forecast, and that things were going to get worse around the time of our flight. I'm sorry to say we didn't heed his warning.

The next portent of trouble came as we passed through security. The security guard, who took our hand-baggage to place it on the conveyor belt that was to take it through the X-ray machine, looked at us with pity in his eyes.

'They've just taken away some of the passengers who arrived on that incoming plane on stretchers,' he said. And he *chuckled*.

I couldn't believe my ears. I decided he must be exaggerating, but it certainly unsettled us. Then as we sat in the departure lounge we heard several announcements regarding other flights being cancelled – but not ours. We seemed destined to fly. The sound of the wind howling around the building was terrifying enough, but through the rain-lashed windows we could see our aircraft, almost lost in the gloom, being buffeted mercilessly by the gusting wind.

The horror of the journey itself, and in particular the landing, almost defies description. Suffice to say that people all around us were being violently sick, and several were screaming. We were holding hands and praying out loud in tongues! I really thought that we might all die that night. I was frantically praying up all the positive scriptures that I could about God's angels being with his people in the storm.

The distress caused by travel sickness is acute. Thankfully, in a flight situation like the one that we went through, it is fairly short-lived. When it comes to seasickness, though, it can seem to go on for an age. They say that there are two stages to seasickness. The first is when you think that you are going to die, and the second is when you wish you could. Our brief horror on that plane was but a pinprick compared to Paul's fourteen-day nightmare of surging seas and hurricane-force winds recorded in Acts 27. It is awesome to think that just when God's servant was pursuing a God-given path to Rome feeling that he was in the centre of God's will, he should face that dreadful storm. But he did. Paul simply trusted God in the midst of the storm.

> We shall steer safely through every storm, so long as our heart is right, our intention fervent, our courage steadfast, and our trust fixed on God.[12]

Most of us will also face storms as we move on in the service of God. The real question is not whether or not storms will come, but rather, when they do, how will we survive? Here are some lessons we can learn from Acts 27.

The perfect storm

For two whole weeks Paul and all on board that ill-fated vessel in the eastern Mediterranean were in the grip of terrifying winds. They were travelling at a time when most mariners of their day would have stayed most definitely at home by their warm, cosy fires. This part of the world was infamous for its winter storms between the months of November and March. Paul and the others would have been only too well aware of this. The storm winds refused to abate and the waves pounded their tiny boat mercilessly. It would have been almost impossible for the crew to move around the ship during this kind of maelstrom, let alone the passengers who would have been pinned to the deck in one place for long periods of time. All on board would have realised that there was the constant danger of capsizing or just plain sinking into one of the massive waves without hope of recovery. Even in today's world of liferafts, search and rescue, radar, radio and emergency location beacons this is a frightening enough scenario, brought powerfully to modern day cinema and television screens by Wolfgang Petersen's film *The Perfect Storm*.

But in the primitive seafaring days of the New Testament it must have been terrible. The storm, with its baying voice and tearing gusts, must have torn at their very sanity. In the minds of ancient sailors in those times a storm at sea very often became a vicious sea monster which they believed had a malevolent will all of its own. Fear, terror and a deep despair would have gripped the minds of the crew and passengers alike. Some of the passengers were probably being taken to Rome for capital trial and possible execution anyway, and so the trip was heavy with foreboding before it even began. Worse was yet to come. For the fourteen nights that the terror raged, most of the 276 people aboard ate nothing. Listen to the way it was described by one who suffered the experience.

> They [*the crew*] lost all control of the ship. It was a cork in the storm...Next day, out on the high seas again and badly damaged by the storm, we dumped the cargo overboard. The third day the sailors lightened the ship further by throwing off all the tackle and provisions. It had been many days since we had seen either sun or stars. Wind and waves were battering us unmercifully, and we lost all hope of rescue (vv. 15–20, *The Message*).

Yet amazingly, in the middle of this situation of despair and hopelessness stood the servant of God, Paul, with a real sense of poise and self-control. No doubt he went through his own private agony of seasickness and being thrown around physically by the force of the storm. He would almost certainly have also called upon God to know why he was there at all. It looked likely that all of them would die and that he might never fulfil the thing he felt God was calling him to do – namely to get to Rome and testify to his faith in front of Caesar (see Acts 23:11). But once he had wrestled out these issues alone with God, he was convinced that God had spoken to him, and that he would see them through.

> [*Paul said*] Last night God's angel stood at my side... saying to me, 'Don't give up, Paul. You're going to stand before Caesar yet – and everybody sailing with you is also going to make it.' So, dear friends, take heart. I believe God will do exactly what he told me. But we are going to shipwreck on some island or other (vv. 23–26, *The Message*).

And that's exactly what happened. The ship was wrecked on the tiny island of Malta, and all aboard it were saved. If you know something of the geography of the area, the size of the Mediterranean Sea, and the comparatively small dimensions of Malta, the whole episode is one long string of miracles. But then, despite the ferocity of the storm, Paul was serving a miracle-working God!

Learning Paul's survival tactics

In some ways it's remarkable that God's servant was on a ship facing a life-threatening storm at all. Having been given divine orders to go to Rome, you would imagine that the way would be 'plain sailing'. But it was not. There was no sign of the Lord walking on the waters to deliver him and his shipmates as was the case with the disciples when they faced a similar, much shorter-lived storm. Nor was Paul able to wake up the slumbering Jesus in the boat as his disciples had done during his earthly ministry so that he could rebuke the wind and the waves. Let's face it – circumstances are not always all that we would like them to be even when we are obeying God. Conditions that may have been faced by disciples in the Gospels do not always equate with we are going through in our present day service of the Lord. How did Paul survive the storm? How did he cope with the apparent disaster that threatened his life as well as his ministry?

A prisoner but not a victim

Well, for a start, he may have been a prisoner on that ship, but he was not a victim. Paul did not allow himself to become victimised, either by the Roman soldiers, or by the threat posed by the storm. In the midst of it all, desperate though the situation seemed, he knew who he was – and he knew whom he served. And he refused to allow himself to be discouraged by circumstances that would seem to suggest otherwise.

There is a very thin line between being a prisoner and being a victim. Paul was certainly a captive, but it seemed at times as if he was acting as the captain. In verses 30 and 31, when Paul saw that certain elements of the crew were trying to escape in the lifeboat, he gave orders to the skipper that if those men did not stay with the ship they would be lost. The 'master' immediately obeyed the man of God, and issued his own orders to that effect.

When God's servant is in the storm, he or she need not be its victim. The real struggle is won or lost in the mind. It is all about attitude. How we perceive ourselves in the midst of the storm really matters. Self-pity, fear, regret... these are all perfectly understandable but can become the enemies of survival.

Terry Waite, a delightful, huge man, who was one-time advisor on international affairs to the then Archbishop of Canterbury, was held hostage in Lebanon for five years. He had gone to the capital of that war-torn land to try to negotiate the release of some other hostages being held against their will. Sadly, Terry was himself captured and held hostage. He was terrorised and on at least one occasion subjected to a mock execution. He never knew from one moment to the next of his terrifying incarceration, whether he would survive to see his homeland again. Once released, however, and during his journey home, he stepped off the plane to face the scrutiny of the world's press who were waiting to interview him. I heard him being interviewed, and was impressed by his answers. In response to a question, Terry spoke to the assembled journalists about what had kept him sane during the long ordeal. After deep thought, which exposed the almost overwhelming emotions within, he said that he had no regrets, no self-pity, no recriminations. That apparently had been his motto throughout the time he was incarcerated, and what stuck in his mind when looking back upon it.

• *No regrets?* Not because it would not be perfectly normal to have them – but because vain regrets can eat away at our peace and sense of well-being in the hands of God. After all, the worst thing we can do is make a mistake that might lead to our death, but then what? An eternal weight of glory? In the case of Paul, he might have had some well-founded regrets about the decisions made by the skipper and the owners of the ship to set sail when they did. He had, after all, warned them of the dangerous path upon which they were embarked. Yet, thank God, his sovereignty covers even our mistakes and the mistakes of others. That boat should not have been at sea at that time of the year, but God is bigger than our errors, and had an appointment for Paul in a distant island.

One remarkable book that sustained me often in facing overwhelming storms is Jerry Bridges' *Trusting God*. In it he comments on our 'if onlys', born out of regret.

> Our lives are...cluttered with a lot of 'if onlys'. 'If only I had done this,' or 'if only that had not happened.' But ...God has no 'if onlys'. God never makes a mistake; God has no regrets. 'As for God, his way is perfect.' (Psalm 18:30). We can trust God. He is trustworthy.[13]

• *No self-pity?* Now that's a hard one. We have already looked at self-pity earlier in this book as we considered how it could hinder our journey to wholeness. But when we set out to serve God we don't expect to get treated so roughly. When I entered the ministry I did so with the highest hopes of serving God and others. I certainly didn't expect to battle with church boards, face the flack of intense personal criticism, and suffer constant isolation and the misunderstanding of my motives. Many who come across these things in the course of their journey of Christian service become discouraged and turn back. Self-pity will turn us into victims if we are not careful. However, God will use us in the storm if our hearts are free from self-pity.

- *No recriminations?* Paul does not seem to have got bitter in the midst of the storm. He was only on this leg of the journey because the captain, his crew and others did not listen to his advice and chose to set sail. Perhaps they didn't fancy the nightlife in Fair Havens! Maybe there were commercial considerations pressing them to make the journey through the dangerous winter months – considerations that outweighed human safety. There was no point going over and over the matter in his mind – just as many centuries later Terry Waite settled *his* mind not to get bitter in his hostage cell – because bitterness saps our inner energy just when we need it most to survive.

Seeing the view from up higher

Near where we live is an area of coast where the fishing is good over a sandy bank in fairly deep water below some cliffs. I love to go there on a friend's fishing boat and wait with our lines out over the bank to see if we can catch various kinds of flat fish. Yet, just occasionally, because the sandbank is near a corner of land, the waters get very choppy there, churned up by the confluence of the tides. Sometimes we feel as though we are just a cork being tossed about on a huge sea as we wait for our elusive bites. At other times I have been to the top of the cliffs nearby to enjoy the view, go for a walk, or buy an ice cream. Then, when I look down upon the area of the sandbank the view is totally different. The waves that really frighten me when I am in our small fishing boat are but a tiny ruffling on an otherwise perfect blue sheet of water. The great distance with which we seem to feel we are separated from the land looks like just a hands breadth to me standing at the top of the cliffs. Now, when we are being subjected to a rough tossing on a fishing trip, I try to remember what the very same situation looks like from up there, and I am comforted by the relative smallness of the waves and the nearness of a landing place.

How did Paul maintain his peace of mind in the midst of the storm? He did so by seeking God's perspective on his situation. Things are not always necessarily just as they seem. It's clear that whilst others were panicking, or shoring up the ship, Paul was seeking the Lord (see vv. 23–26). He might have been subject to criticism for his other-worldly approach to the crisis. Yet he chose this particular plan of action because he knew that the eternal God always sees everything from the throne, and the view from there is different. Paul understood the truth that led him to pen the words of Romans 8:28: 'And we know that in all things God works for the good of those who love him, who have been called according to his purpose.' Paul had learnt that truth on the high seas.

God is always working for our eternal good, if we love him and are called according to his purpose. This does not give us all the answers, but does give us the confidence that there is no chaos in heaven. Though it

would have seemed incredible to the average member
of that ship's crew or passenger list, God had a purpose
in the storm. He was blowing the ship to Malta. He had
an appointment for Paul with Publius, the Roman chief
official, whose father was desperately ill. The healing
of Publius' father became the start of the church in
that land. (See my earlier teaching about a different
perspective.)

Remembering the name in the label

One of the lessons I have learnt from frequent visits to
hospital over the last few years is that if you want to
keep track of your possessions, especially your clothes,
you have to make sure that your name is clearly and
indelibly marked in them. If this is ignored or avoided,
the chances are that they will disappear, never to be
seen again. We must remember that as God's special
people, we are not going to suffer the same fate! We
will not be lost without trace. In Isaiah 43:1–7, the Lord
sets out his sovereign care for those who serve him.

But now, this is what the LORD says – he who created you,
O Jacob, he who formed you, O Israel: Fear not, for I have
redeemed you; I have summoned you by name; you are
mine. When you pass through the waters, I will be with
you; and when you pass through the rivers, they will not
sweep over you. When you walk through the fire, you
will not be burned; the flames will not set you ablaze. For
I am the LORD, your God, the Holy One of Israel, your
Saviour; I give Egypt for your ransom, Cush and Seba in
your stead. Since you are precious and honoured in my
sight, and because I love you, I will give men in exchange
for you, and people in exchange for your life. Do not be
afraid, for I am with you; I will bring your children from
the east and gather you from the west. I will say to the

north, 'Give them up!' and to the south, 'Do not hold them back.' Bring my sons from afar and my daughters from the ends of the earth – everyone who is called by my name, whom I created for my glory, whom I formed and made.

It is clear from verse 7 that God has called us by his name – that we are each marked with that name on the label. Paul also kept his cool in the storm by reminding himself of who he belonged to. When describing his encounter with the angel of God to the rest of the passengers and crew, he calls God 'whose I am and whom I serve' (Acts 27:23). He had a high sense of who he was. He was not on that ship by accident. Neither was he heading for Rome because he had broken the law. He was the Lord's, and it was the Lord who had brought him this difficult way.

We will do well to remember that we are not just helpless victims of pain, or at the whim of some cruel employer, or being pressed by harsh and unyielding circumstances. We belong to the King of kings, and are sons and daughters of the living God. God needs witnesses in storms. He also has to sometimes use high winds to redirect our otherwise slightly askew journeying to fulfil his divine appointments. Yes, Paul was called to go to Rome, but he was also going to be used by God in Malta. The two causes did not need to be mutually exclusive.

Remembering who's in charge

Paul also remained calm in the midst of this dreadful experience by choosing to believe what God had said more than the evidence of his immediate circumstances. He had no evidence for what he told the crew other than what he had heard from the Lord (see v. 25). Yet this was sufficient for Paul. The deed was done as far as he was concerned, because God had spoken.

His faith was not *in faith*. He was not saying in effect, 'Because I believe this strongly enough I will disregard what plain common sense shows me.' No. He had heard from God and was prepared to trust him. Nor was his faith in a person. There were no human resources left to them. They had despaired of rescue. There was no lifeboat to call, and no coastguard. But he had the word of the Lord, and so he had peace. (See my earlier teaching on resting on a word from God.)

Refusing to stay silent

There was one further element of the way Paul went through that storm and emerged victorious. Despite being a passenger on his way to be tried before Caesar – a virtual remand prisoner – and notwithstanding the fact that he had no real position of power or influence on board the ship, Paul refused to be silent. Throughout the storm he continued to speak out for God. In fact, this became a secret of success for Paul which went on throughout his subsequent house arrest in Rome. He never regarded imprisoning circumstances as reason enough to be silent. He was constantly on the lookout for an audience, and God sent them to him.

Paul was a witness despite the difficult situation. He witnessed boldly throughout the ordeal. What he had to say was not just a 'four things God wants you to know' type of pre-packaged sermonising. He didn't just give out tracts. When we lived in Zimbabwe there were groups of zealous Christian young people who used to race around the country in pick-up trucks on their way to camps and conventions. On the way they shoved handfuls of tracts out of the windows of the speeding vehicles whenever they passed crowds of people at bus stops or traffic halts. They were keen, and meant well, but they were not necessarily 'witnessing'. Paul witnessed by being a mouthpiece for God to people in crisis. He brought a 'now' word from the Lord to people with whom he shared a common struggle. From a position of vulnerability and personal need, he spoke as one who had heard from God. True witnessing always comes from that direction. Like Ezekiel, who sat silent where the captives sat for a long time before ever he spoke out to them in a prophetic sense, we need to earn the right to speak for God. One of my favourite definitions of evangelism is 'one beggar telling another beggar where to find bread'.

When he did speak out, Paul's words were carefully chosen. He spoke in warnings, clearly given. In Acts 27:10 he warned them that if they pursued the course of setting sail, the journey would be a disaster. Again in verse 31 he warned the centurion that if his men made off in the lifeboat, they would perish. This element of warning is often missing in modern evangelism, especially the increasingly popular (and rightly so) friendship evangelism. Paul withheld nothing of the mind of God from them, even when what he had to share was mainly bad news.

Being a Barnabas

Throughout the ordeal by storm, Paul also maintained his cool by determining to live a positive lifestyle. He was constantly encouraging others. Verses 33 to 36 show him urging them all to eat, and encouraging them all in their hope of deliverance. He would not enter into despair. He maintained a thankful, praising heart, giving thanks for the meagre rations with which they broke their fast on the eve of their shipwreck. Praying over mouldy grain and damp ship's biscuits must have seemed strange indeed! Yet, it is a key to surviving the storms we encounter in the will of God if we can remain thankful for small things, and give thanks in all things. Even the very act of eating, for Paul, became a statement of faith. 'Eat up!' he called. 'You're going to need all your strength to survive what's coming!' Paul's ministry of encouragement was not just in what he said, but in the example he set. It was also very practical encouragement, taking note of the physical need for food among those whom he knew were facing impending shipwreck.

Despite my pain I have really done my best to remain aware of the needs of others and to be a 'Barnabas' wherever possible. He is the New Testament Christian leader who was given that name because it means 'son of encouragement'. It must have been so difficult for Paul to retain his focus on meeting the needs of others because his own needs were so great, but he felt keenly the heart of God's compassion towards his fellow strugglers with the sea.

Knowing God is there

In Acts 27 and 28 Paul was in deep trouble both on the ship and even after the wreck and his arrival on shore. When he went out to gather sticks to light a fire to warm the others (a great picture of him serving others despite his own discomfort), a snake jumped out of the fire and bit him. Satan often oversteps the mark. What he intended for evil, God used for good. The islanders saw the deliverance which God gave his servant in that attack, and the door for evangelising a whole new community was wide open. When the Lord delivered Paul from the storm and from the snake, then the islanders were ready to receive his words. The apostle would never have chosen either event. He would have preferred to travel at a quieter time of the year. He would certainly have avoided picking up the snake if he had seen it. But God had a higher plan in taking his servant through both situations. Seasick or snake-bitten, he was still the witness God knew he would be.

Through this entire terrible storm, Paul was not alone. That is one of the clearest lessons to come from these incidents. Though the boat was hundreds of kilometres from land, and was tossed by terrible seas in the blackest of nights, Paul was not alone. He was hearing from God. He received angelic visitation. When he prayed and called upon the Lord, God spoke to him. His sense of the presence of God was unbroken, even by the wind and the waves.

Some years ago, I was working in a mining town as the pastor of a local Pentecostal church. I had the opportunity to go underground in the town's last surviving coalmine. The coalface was more than a mile deep, and nearly five miles out under the seabed! The journey down there was long and exhausting, and I was grateful that as a visitor I was not expected to begin a long working shift on my arrival. A remarkable truth became clear to me down there. Despite the distance from the surface, God was in that place. Several of the men in my congregation had come to know Jesus whilst working underground. God had heard their prayers of repentance five miles under the sea.

One lady, then a widow, told of how her husband had heard the voice of God calling to him after an explosion in the pit had sealed off some of the tunnels. Her husband heard the voice giving clear but unusual instructions, even in those terrible circumstances.

'Go deeper!' the voice had said, when everything in his natural instincts urged him to head for the surface. He became one of only three survivors, when over a hundred other men died in the pit accident that day. But didn't the writer of Psalm 139 say, 'if I make my bed in the depths, you are there' (v. 8). So when God's servant Paul was facing powerful contrary storm-force winds, he remained in fellowship with God.

Perhaps in those difficult circumstances, Paul was made aware of the truth of God's presence with his persecuted and troubled people in the days of Old Testament. As a scholar of the ancient Hebrew texts, Paul would have known well the promises of Isaiah 43:1 and 2. These words would have given comfort to Paul as he wrestled with seasickness and the fear of death. He would also have known the story from the book of Daniel of the three young men who suffered persecution because of their trust in the God of Israel. They knew that the God they served could deliver them, but if not, they determined not to bow down to the idol erected by the Babylonian king, and so were condemned to be thrown into the furnace of fire. As they were bound and tossed into the cremation flames, the soldiers whose task it was to execute them were themselves overcome by the intensity of the fire. Yet, amazingly to those who looked on, the three young men were able to walk about free in the flames, and there appeared to be a fourth person in there with them. The king, Nebuchadnezzar, exclaimed, 'Look, I see four men walking around in the fire, unbound and unharmed, and the fourth looks like a son of the gods' (Dan. 3:25). He was nearly right! The fourth may either have been an angel or perhaps a 'theophany' – a pre-incarnation appearance in bodily form of the second Person of the Trinity. God was with his servants when they faced the fires of persecution.

Recently, a speaker at our church encouraged the people to go away into the week and reckon that God had put them in the situations they find themselves in. We were told to sit at our desk or at the wheel of our car or truck and say to ourselves: 'I am here by Divine appointment.' I have had to do that many times in a hospital bed and it is not easy. It was not easy for Paul, either. But he would have taken heart from knowing that he was only on board that boat because of his obedience to God.

Perhaps you are only in that church because you obeyed God's call? Or maybe you are only working in that country or on that factory floor because God put you there? You may only have entered that relationship because you had a sense of Divine leading. When the fires rage, and storm winds blow, don't forget that he is with you; know that God is there.

Conclusion

In both the Old and the New Testament it continues to be a theme of Scripture that God's servants will face trials and storms of all sorts and sizes. If we are following a Lord and master who was himself rejected and finally crucified by those whom he tried to serve lovingly and sacrificially, it is hardly surprising that we will face opposition too. Jesus warned his followers, 'Remember the words I spoke to you: "No servant is greater than his master." If they persecuted me, they will persecute you also' (Jn. 15:20a).

There were occasions in the Gospels when Jesus himself sent his disciples into the face of the most appalling storms, some of which even threatened to overwhelm the most seasoned of fishermen. They had obeyed his command, only to be faced by life-threatening consequences. Likewise, Job was a man of God. Yet God allowed him to suffer for a reason he couldn't see. And yet, from his story we can see that he chose to trust in God, treasure his Word, worship, and pray. Clearly, choices make a difference in our suffering. And the events recorded in Acts 27 give us some good pointers to keeping our cool when we hit storms in following what we believe to be God's will for us.

- We may be prisoners in our circumstances, but we don't have to be victims.
- We can avoid regrets, self-pity and recriminations.
- We can look for God's perspective on the situation.
- We can remind ourselves of who we are in Christ.
- We can choose to believe what God has said more than the evidence of our difficult circumstances.
- We can refuse to be silenced, boldly speaking out for God in all situations.
- We can live a positive lifestyle, giving thanks for all things and encouraging others.
- We can reckon that God is with us no matter how desperate our circumstances and even when things appear to get worse!

Part Four

Shepherding the Sick

Introduction

I love the local church. I always have and I hope I always will. Like Bill Hybels, Senior Pastor at Willow Creek Community Church in Chicago, I believe the local church is the hope of the world. Para-church organisations and missions have their place but the local church is still God's 'plan A'. Jesus loved the church and gave himself for it. But the church is not always all it should be. No one knows that quite as well as someone who has pastored churches on two continents over thirty-plus years.

I also know what it feels like to be in pain and in church. Often that has meant feeling like I just did not belong there, that I was an embarrassment to the people there, or that I should even leave. I know that others feel the same way. When I was taking part in a recent phone-in programme on a Christian radio station a lady called in to say that she had taken her disabled son to as many as ten different churches only to be driven to leave each one by the attitudes of the believers towards her son. It is appalling that a community which God created to be an incubator of nurture and care should become a hostile and threatening place to people in pain.

This subject is of special relevance to the Pentecostal and charismatic wing of the church in which I have spent my entire ministry. We are very good at offering prayer for healing and expecting God to work miracles. I have always been involved in the ministry of healing and still am today. Jesus said that those who follow him will lay hands upon the sick and they shall recover. Christians who are sick are instructed in James 5 to call for the elders of the church whose task it is anoint them with oil and to pray over them the prayer of faith so that the sick will be healed. Each of these things I do and have had done to me, expecting results. However, it is true to say that large numbers of people seek healing prayer and see no outward or immediate sign of things being different. Yet I believe it is still right to lay hands upon the sick and receive such prayer. *Something* happens when we do, even if we can't see it.

Problems come for many in this environment when they are not healed. Intense pressure can come upon them as a result. It is hard enough to cope with the disappointment of not seeing your prayers answered in the way that you had hoped, without having to carry the added weight of other people's criticism and in some cases rejection too. Churches in this particular section of the Christian community need to find ways of lifting that pressure off suffering individuals. They need to help them to cope with their pain and suffering in the period leading up to their healing, and need to be supportive – even if they are not healed at all.

This is a fallen world, and we live in the in-between period of the 'now and not yet' of the kingdom of God. The kingdom of God has come in Christ, and all the wonderful good news of the gospel is there for us to proclaim, but the full effect of Christ's victory over sickness in particular will only come at the time of the

Second Coming. I know some will disagree with that statement, and they are entitled to their view, believing that it was all done 2,000 years ago and all we need to do now to be healed is to claim that. But please be aware that it will be very difficult for honest suffering Christians to be around these people.

None of this needs to be. If churches will open their eyes to the needs of the suffering around them as well as in the developing world they will see real opportunities to reflect God's love to his creation. In this part we will look at some of the ways that churches can serve those in pain amongst them whilst they wait for their healing.

1

Practical Care

Three lessons learned

I remain deeply grateful to the medical teams in Intensive Care who kept me alive and looked after me at my lowest points. Their devotion, not just to the patient, but to maintaining frontline hi-tech training standards, has brought many sufferers back from the brink. In retrospect, I have asked myself what could have been done to make the whole experience any easier for myself or my family. There are some practical lessons I have learned, and they may be relevant for anyone who has a seriously ill friend or relative in hospital.

Prayer for the patient

Firstly, Christian friends and churches need to recognise that this kind of situation is a spiritual battle as much as a physical one, and that their urgent imploring prayers do really count. People who cared for me, who were prevented from visiting, came and stood outside the ICU in nearby corridors without drawing attention to themselves. And there, they prayed. Consequently, they felt part of the crisis without being directly in contact with me.

When crises occur, those most closely involved cannot really pray. Their emotions are in turmoil, and
their minds occupied with just coping. This is one of
those times when they simply cannot climb any great
spiritual mountains. The prayers of others can carry
them through. We know that a sovereign God is in
charge, but he has delegated to his people the task of
doing warfare with the powers of darkness. In cases like
mine, the battle really is one of life and death. I owe a
great debt to those who 'prayed me through', and so
urge others to take up this kind of active intercession
for those passing through such deep waters.

Ministry in hospital

Secondly, I feel a real burden of concern for the staff
of the thousands of intensive care beds around the
country. They bear a heavy responsibility of care for
the critically ill and the dying, together with their
families. Shortly after my own crisis, and just before
my discharge from hospital, I asked a porter to wheel
me from the general ward to the ICU in a wheelchair. I
wanted to see where I had fought my battles all those
weeks, but I also wanted to thank the team there. The
charge nurse told me that when I was well again, he
would appreciate an occasional pastoral visit by me to
the Unit. He felt that this could benefit relatives and
staff alike. He said that they lacked pastoral or spiritual
input, with most chaplains and ministers passing
the Unit by. He suspected that the highly technical
atmosphere of the place probably scared chaplains – it
certainly scared me!

I know that some units are quite unwelcoming
because of the seriousness of the business going on
inside. The relatives' room, however, is usually full of

needy folk, and often charged with emotion. The staff restroom too might be a place where an occasional concerned inquiry from a caring pastor might make a difference.

Maybe churches could take on board the idea of praying for their local ICU, letting it be known to the staff that pastoral care is available for them too. They handle life and death daily and need all the support they can get as long as it is offered in a careful, kind and gracious way, without intrusion.

Support for relatives

A third lesson I have learned about practical care is how important it is to belong to the right kind of local church when a crisis happens. Diane was never alone when she arrived at the hospital. At that particular time in her life – the time I have shared with you – she was also fighting a battle with terrible pain because of sciatica and was often confined to a wheelchair herself, but amazing friends and fellow believers were always on hand to wheel her to my bedside. Whether or not she was wheelchair-bound, she was always accompanied by someone from our home church or a nearby fellowship. It was nerve-wracking enough for her to arrive not knowing what she would find, but the comfort of another's presence was a great blessing. These tactful, caring friends always seemed to know when to withdraw and leave us alone. At times they would just sit with her, holding my spare hand, and pray silently. Our friend Sandie, whose husband had died not long before my decade of pain began, became our greatest help. She was always there for us, night or day, when we needed her. A trained nurse, she literally saved my life on one occasion when she spotted that I had stopped breathing.

Back at home there were people to talk football with my son, wash floors, whisk the ironing away and bring ready-cooked meals. What a fellowship! You need never be lonely if you become part of a New Testament-style church. The sad fact is that this is not always the experience that people have with church when passing through prolonged periods of pain.

The problem of loneliness

Loneliness is the darker side of the planet Pain. It is seldom subject to the same kind of scrutiny and publicity that pain itself receives, but yet is nonetheless real. Only the person going through it really understands the full nature of their problem. Cut off from social activities, sometimes from work, often from friends, pain sufferers plough a lonely furrow. Some welcome that kind of isolation, preferring to lick their wounds privately, out of the gaze of others. That was not how it affected me.

Although I have mentioned above how my wife and I were (and are) blessed today to be part of a very loving fellowship that gave and continues to give wonderful support, it is true to say that we have indeed experienced different levels of church care during my decade of pain. I remember those early days when I was first ill. The phone went quiet. I grieved over the loss of relationships. The doorbell virtually rusted over, the battery going flat without anyone noticing! Colleagues who once sought my opinion were conspicuous by their absence. Very few called to see me. Of those who did, even fewer really ministered to me. One local minister came occasionally, but never prayed nor offered to pray. Perhaps he was embarrassed by my situation and intimidated by our professional relationship. It was as if

I became an embarrassment to leaders committed to the culture of success that pervades the charismatic church. They appeared to support me... but from a distance.

Having said all that, I am deeply grateful for those who telephoned from all over the world, with offers of prayer support. I have also had the joy of spending some years in a church where I became the pastor with the church *knowing* that I was unwell and yet still willing to support me. Over the long period of my battle with this dreadful disease they have shown me a different way of 'being church'. They are a truly loving kind of community of God's people, committed to one another in reality and love, for as long as it takes. We have come to see through their persistent, practical, loving care, that when the Christian church functions as it was designed to do, it can be such a force for comfort and healing to those who suffer life's deepest pains.

Pain isolates its victims, so that every source of outside help seems to require a major effort. Part of the shock of a painful condition that sets in for the long term is the realisation that you are largely on your own. Of course, for the Christian believer there is always the comfort that we know God is with us. Yet, in time of pain, it is a daily discipline to remind yourself of this fact. You start to feel that you are a nuisance at the doctor's surgery. The local chemist sighs as he hands over yet another prescription for even stronger painkillers. Friends and acquaintances stop asking how you are, afraid of the long litany of woe that may follow. They keep you at a distance because they too are afraid of this monster 'pain' that stalks in the dark. Theirs is a genuine fear that if it could happen to you it could also happen to them.

Families may begin to withdraw over the long haul, too. Your anxious loved ones, hoping against hope for a miracle with you, begin to realise that normal family life is unlikely to resume soon. You sense their sadness and disappointment, unable to give them the good news for which they long. You run into work colleagues who offer unhelpful comments like 'Aren't you better yet?' or who offer various home remedies like copper amulets and herbal potions. Or else they warn you in grave tones that the boss is getting pretty fed up with your repeated absences and that you had better get back pretty soon. Yes, you're on your own all right!

I have learnt all this the hard way yet I am convinced that no Christian should have to suffer pain alone. It need not be like this. There are ways to cope with pain; we don't need to be just its victims, we can fight back, and in many cases, overcome. The community of God's people was created in the heart of God so that no one in pain should be alone. There is more to healing than the alleviation of symptoms. The reason for the very existence of the church is that it should be a fountain of life and healing, and a place of support in times of crisis and need. Approached in the right way and with the right kind of support from the church, all the effects of pain can be managed so as to minimise their destructive power.

Just being there

I remember once, I was driving a one-ton Toyota truck at the highest speed possible for the road conditions. The word 'road' would be a generous description for the meandering, undulating rocky track that stretched ahead of me into the African night. It was after dark, and I was there in defiance of the mission's rule which required that expatriate mission drivers should not use the dirt roads at night. The reason for this prohibition

was that the hospital and mission were located on
the border between Zimbabwe and Mozambique in
southern Africa. At that time, Mozambique was in the
grip of a particularly brutal and bloody war, and there
were frequent incursions by guerrilla soldiers across
the border. The very real risk was that there might be
terrorists near the isolated track, who may try to stop
mission drivers in order to commandeer the vehicle.
What they would then do with one spare European
driver did not bear thinking about. So my late-night
struggle with the steering wheel of my bucking truck
was ill-advised – but it was also necessary.

The reason why it was necessary was that I was on
my way to the remote mission hospital. I was going
there in order to deliver an urgent message to one of
the expatriate missionary medical staff. News had come
to us in the city that her father, back home in the UK,
had been taken seriously ill. It was unlikely that the
workers at the rural hospital compound would radio
in for some days, and we had no other quick means
of contacting them. Other methods of transmitting
messages, mainly involving sending runners on local
buses, would take a long time to get through and were
not guaranteed to arrive at all.

Having delivered my message, and made arrangements
for the nurse concerned to use the radio phone to call
her family, I didn't wait around – I set off straight away
for home again. By this time, there were definite signs
of a gathering thunderstorm. But I had left my wife
and then small son at home in the rather vulnerable
suburb where we lived. The minefield of the border
ran very near our back garden. The local neighbours
used to run a 'neighbourhood watch' scheme, armed
with semi-automatic rifles! I did not really trust them
to be able to defend our home without me being there,

and so did not hang around out in the bush. I knew that my family would also feel quite uncomfortable in the vivid kind of lightning storms which are common in that part of Africa, one of which was obviously on its way.

Then the storm broke. The road, which was normally strewn with potholes, piles of gravel and small rocks, quickly became a raging torrent of brown water. This made it virtually impossible for me to see the way, so I moved forward gingerly, always keeping my foot ready for the brake pedal. Around me the black skies flashed intermittently with that haunting sheet lightning so typical of an African storm. On one occasion when the lightning flashed, I crested a ridge on the track. At that moment I could see for miles across the barren African landscape. I was absolutely and completely alone. There was not another living creature within miles... or so it seemed. I realised how extremely vulnerable I was. If I'd had one of the very frequent punctures that were part of our regular lives, I would have had to repair it myself. Changing a wheel in that isolated location, I would soon have found out if there *were* other living things around! If the truck got bogged down in the mud, I would be on my own for the night. If the worst happened and I missed the road and overturned, no one was coming to my rescue.

Throughout the trip, I kept up a vigil of horizon-watching, as well as staring at the ruts in which I was driving. I have never felt more alone in all my life. But I knew that God was with me and would protect me. That was the basis of my confidence, even though the situation was fraught with danger. The journey had been undertaken for humanitarian purposes, and I was only in the country because of God's call on my life. Those facts, however, served only to dull, not remove, the fear of being alone.

Nor was my relief ever greater than when I hit the tarmac that night. When the dirt road ended, and the lovely smooth tar began, it felt like being lifted on angel's wings and carried along. Subsequently, after long hours of driving fast, I arrived at our city home to a relieved welcome from my wife and son, and the dog.

The 'alone-ness' I had felt that night had been new to me. I was not to know it again for quite a long time – that is, until I got ill. Pain and sickness have a way of making the sufferer feel completely and utterly alone. Yes, we know that God is with us, and derive peace from that fact. As the storm rages around us, though, we can feel so isolated and vulnerable. It is my belief that we will only truly be able to minister to people who are facing such storms if we recognise the isolating nature of severe suffering and trauma and do our utmost to alleviate it in any way that we can.

I have already mentioned that perhaps one of the loneliest experiences in the world is to be taken along a hospital corridor on a trolley towards an operating theatre. No one else can go there for you. Your spouse or loved ones may even accompany you to the theatre door, but as you enter the dreaded portals, you are on your own. Prior to my own experience of major pancreatic surgery, one of the senior resident doctors had come to see me just before the porters arrived. He was a Christian, and sensing how afraid I might be, had come back to pray for me. He parted the curtains that had been drawn around my bed, where I lay dressed (or undressed) in the undignified garb of the preoperative procedures, and came inside. His prayer was very special, and reminded me that God has his people in every situation, and can meet us at the hour of our greatest need. I have always made a point since then of popping in to see church members just prior to their 'going down' for surgery if I can possibly do so.

Sometimes the greatest service a Christian or a church can offer someone in long-term trials and pain is to just be there for them. Some years ago, Diane's mother had a heart attack and went through a prolonged period of nervous symptoms and disability as a result of it. The pastor of her church at that time, Cecil Jarvis, was a really gracious and loving man. He knew that he had no easy answers, and I know he did not feel like a miracle-worker. Yet he just kept coming, faithfully and at regular intervals to sit with Diane's mum in silence and spend some time with her, always offering to pray for her when he left. Because of that, and the love of husband, daughters and other folk from the Christian community, she was never alone. I am glad of that, as I myself have since learnt the true meaning of the word 'alone' and it is not an easy thing to bear.

The local church has a great responsibility here and must not overlook those at the margins of the church. Being part of a non-Christian family can cause additional problems when people are in pain, as can living in rural or isolated areas. There is a real danger that churches which are very much geared up to meet the needs of the regular attendees and those who meet in home groups might overlook the needs of the less committed, or those who are unable to regularly attend because of work, family or other issues. I have found that this is particularly true in a larger fellowship, and we have put in place systems to try and prevent this. Regular meetings of the pastoral team to try and spot absentees and gather information about folk in need are one method. I have even heard of a large church which actually videos the entrance porch and then allocates a team member to review the tape on a Monday to

see who was missing. Even in a smaller church folk
can slip through the net, and it is so important to set
care in place by delegating responsibility for being
aware of people's needs to suitably gifted and called
individuals. Sometimes the newly retired can serve a
pastor and church in this kind of capacity and can be a
key resource for covering some of the gaps.

So being there is important. Just be there!

Setting the solitary in families

The isolation of people who are passing through storms
can and must be addressed at its root. Suffering people
need people, not theories, nor even theologies of the
'blessings' of suffering. They need people who love
them, and who feel for them in their trials. But they
also need people who will hope with them and for
them until they come through, or for as long as it takes.
God has given us people like that. Not many, but they
are there, and we thank him for them. He truly does
set the solitary in families (see Ps. 68:6, KJV).

This truth first came to my attention during a period
in our ministry when my wife Diane was very ill with
depression and was coping with withdrawal from
addictive tranquilliser drugs. We also had our small son
Matthew, and I was facing very heavy responsibilities
in the church we were leading. At that time, God
challenged me as to the true purpose of the honey
cell in the life of bees. Cells exist, I realised with fresh
insight, to provide a source of food and nurture for the
young bees during their vulnerable early stages. They
were not just created to give us something sweet to
put on our toast. They have a nurturing function, and
the sweetness of honey is the result of it. God wants
the church to be a network of life cells, or honey cells

like in a honeycomb, so that those who haven't been Christians for too long, or who are in special need of nurture and care, can receive care.

It was at the time of our particular need that three ladies had turned up at our house declaring that they felt God was calling them to become our own 'honey cell' to pray Diane through this crisis. For nearly two years they met with her regularly. They were always available on the end of a telephone day or night. They were never judgemental and always prayed with faith even when things looked so bleak. They truly offered Diane a life cell of hope.

We all need small accountability and support groups like that when we are in the middle of storms. The best time to prepare them is before the weather gets really bad in the first place. One of the best things we can do for needy folk is to set them in small groups of truly caring, praying friends of the same sex. Instead of leaving them on their own to fend for themselves, we can take seriously the vision of the church as a network of life-giving cells, bringing nurture and healing to those in need.

Using self-help groups

Whilst illness and pain, then, are very isolating experiences, I am convinced that there is no need to suffer them alone. In fact, the presence of others, and especially people who have gone through the same thing before, can be a great encouragement. That would be the difference between the sort of support cell such as I have described above and a self-help group. One is made up of a few chosen, trusted individuals, who may or may not have been through similar trials themselves; the other, the self-help group, is made up of past sufferers, a little on the lines of Alcoholics Anonymous and similar groups. These kinds of groups do have limitations, and must avoid becoming 'pity parties', but they can also be a source of great strength, drawn mainly from the knowledge that others have been there too.

During my experiences in Africa, and particularly as part of the mission hospital team, I became aware of the very different attitude towards suffering in that culture. No individual was ever left alone. Their families would usually bring them to the hospital, and then stay with them. They camped around the compound, and made meals for their sick loved one. Sometimes a close family member would actually camp under the patient's bed! Sickness is a family event in the Third World. So is bereavement and grief. We seek privacy for these things in the West, and often suffer a good deal of loneliness as a result. In Africa, for instance, there are very few mental institutions and old folk's homes. People needing that type of care are looked after by their family, or in the village setting. This kind of extended family, however, is under great strain where the dreadful disease AIDS is taking its toll. In some villages, virtually all the parents are being wiped out, and huge numbers of AIDS orphans are being created as a result. This modern-day plague is putting great pressure of family life and old fashioned standards of care. But there are still real lessons for us in the West to learn.

So often, sadly, when we are fighting illness or trauma there is little or no help from family or friends. Elderly infirm are shunted into nursing homes. Terminally ill are put into hospital to see out their days. A clinical exclusion zone is extended around the seriously ill, and families and friends are all too often outside of

it. In my own case I gained tremendous help from the
community of the church where we worshipped as a
family. It was and is a real community, and it proved
to be a lifesaver for us.

Such an environment gives at least an opportunity
where folk can talk about what is going on and share
the sufferer's pain. I read about some research which
showed that there can be a measurable benefit from
that kind of care and support. Apparently, in one study
of women who had breast cancer, those who attended
a mutual support group at least once a week for a year,
felt better and lived almost two years longer than the
women who did not attend the group. Both groups
of patients also received the same chemotherapy and
radiation treatment.[14] In any case, whether the benefits
of such care can be measured or not, they are a very
useful piece of equipment in the toolbox of survival
tactics for coping with hard times. The whole concept
of shared pain is something fairly unusual outside the
human race. It can be observed in animals, I think,
though usually only between a parent and offspring
type of situation. Amongst human beings, however, like
the proverb says – a problem shared can be a problem
halved.

Emotional Care

The importance of touch

The strength that human beings draw from each other in times of pain and difficulty is remarkable. The effect that the touch of another person's hand can have came home to me clearly when I was in the ICU. I found that although I was intensely weak and in pain, and often comatose, I gained real comfort from the hands of the nurses who took my pulse during the regular observations. Blood pressure can be read these days with minimal attention from the nurse. They just wrap the cuff quickly around the patient's arm, and then press a button on a machine. It inflates the cuff and produces the digital reading, which is then read off by the nurse. Temperature readings are done in a moment by pointing a kind of ray gun at the ear and pressing the trigger. All well and good, and very efficient, but some of the contact between patient and carer has been lost. But in the taking of the pulse, however, outside of being hooked up to electronic monitors, there is usually a time when the carer is literally holding the patient's wrist, even if only with a couple of fingers. I found myself longing for that contact, and greatly heartened by it. I savoured those thirty seconds of human contact as if it were a three-course meal! Also, during my time in Intensive Care, while I was unable to move my hands, which were pinned down by tubes and wires, Diane found a lovely way of enabling close contact. She used to stand at the end of the bed and put the soles of my feet against her tummy. I could push against her, feel her warmth, and she could gently massage my feet. These momentary contacts all built up my sense of well-being, if nothing else, and made the pain more bearable. Nobody should be left untouched or be made to feel untouchable in their suffering.

This is, of course, part of the idea behind the wonderful hospice movement, founded by Dame Cicely Saunders. She and her colleagues had a concern for patients who were terminally ill with very painful conditions. They did not want them to die alone, or in pain. Hospices now offer the kind of relief and comfort that once were denied to so many dying patients. A large part of the treatment is just the presence and the touch of the team of carers. 'It is not good,' says God in Genesis 1, 'for the man [*or the woman*] to be alone.' Never is that more true than we are in trouble or pain.

This is also part of what lies behind the biblical command to lay hands upon people who are sick or in need when we pray for them. People need to be touched and held. In so doing we break down one of the very real taboos, certainly in British society. In Britain if we brush up against somebody accidentally in the street or on the Underground, we immediately apologise. It seems that touch is seen as a no-go area, and even the shaking of hands as a way of greeting has largely disappeared. It is as if we have offended against something very sacred by invading people's private space. When we touch the sick, we break those barriers down.

When we lay hands on the needy we also identify with them very closely in their problems. By touching them and holding them we are in effect saying 'your problem is my problem.' In a similar way, at that moment our faith and prayer becomes theirs. So we can see just how important the laying on of hands really is. Doing so does not have to be a very religious moment. We can just take someone's hand whilst we pray, or put an arm around their shoulder. People need touch, and prayer for them by the church should include thoughtful touch if at all possible.

Learning how to relax in God's love

Churches should be places of real rest. Not that you would think it by reading the notice sheet or newsletter of most growing evangelical churches. Sometimes the frenetic activity of church life can actually add to a sufferer's pain. It can make it difficult for people to feel that they *really* belong if they don't function at the level of busyness that they see around them. Yet people need to relax as part of their church and Christian experience. As part of the emotional care of the sick and suffering, churches should offer relaxation and model it too.

Proper relaxation is treatment. Resting can actually be a storm-survival tactic. It does give us power over our illnesses. Rest was God's invention, despite all the hype of the good old Protestant work ethic. It is at the heart of God's creative purposes for us – it's called 'Sabbath' – resting.

'Sabbath' any day

The real meaning of Sabbath took me years to understand. I began my Christian life with a fairly typical evangelical outlook that the Christian Sunday was a straight replacement for the Jewish Sabbath (Saturday) and that there was a long shopping list of rules and regulations that controlled it. A Christian was not able to do anything that seemed remotely like fun on a Sunday – watch television, go swimming, play sports for instance, or anything that caused someone else to work. These latter included simple pastimes like eating in a restaurant, going shopping or even just buying a newspaper. Along with these taboos was a list of other 'Thou shalt nots' which came under the heading 'Things that would cause others to stumble' and might cover eating an ice cream in a public place, hanging out washing on the line to dry, and certainly anything else which even looked like having a good time.

Yet these tribal taboos amongst evangelicals are not at all what God intended when he created 'Sabbath' and rested on the seventh day of his creation. Instead he was building into his creative work a principle of rest which continues to this day. All productive living requires a rhythm of work and rest that implies a God-like need to recharge after a busy season. Churches should demonstrate this to an unbelieving community.

There is, of course, also a deep theological meaning to Sabbath that has primarily to do with resting in Christ for our salvation as opposed to trusting in our own good works to make us right with God. 'Sabbath' is the observance of a divinely ordained cycle of work and rest, expending and restoring, giving and receiving, labour and celebration. This is something that many Western Christian leaders and workers do not really understand, let alone experience on a regular basis.

I remember attending a conference for ministers when I was a recent graduate from Bible College. I found myself collecting morning coffee alongside two men whom I regarded as giants of Christian service. These were mighty men of God, role models who had served all their lives in the church. As I listened to their conversation, I became aware that they were boasting to one another that they had never taken a day off in their entire ministry! I could hardly believe my ears, as I was really committed to taking at least one day a week to be with my young wife, even though we had no children at that stage. Yet these men were simply products of their age and culture. They believed in only work and no rest. Yet God has ordained rest as an important part of regular routine.

Sabbath rest is also the freedom to be still and know God. It is an invitation to enjoy God's gracious creation in nature, just as he did himself at the beginning. It is an opportunity to rest in his acceptance and grace, and does not need to be weekly event, or reserved for a few months every seven years. We need to practise daily what it means to cease from our own labours and enjoy relaxing in God's love.

There are good 'vibes' and helpful chemicals released into our tortured systems when we learn to relax properly. Of course, as with other forms of alternative medicine, there are charlatans in the relaxation business. There are people making a great deal of money out of so-called relaxation techniques (some of which are nothing more than common sense when you start to examine them). Nevertheless, those who can perfect the art of relaxation, and practise it daily, will soon start to feel the benefits. Suffering will no longer be their master, and they will begin to hope that things may improve.

The benefits of Sabbath

Along with this there will other benefits for the Christian who learns to enter into the principle of Sabbath and rest.

- *Endurance.* Because we want to serve God long-term, and run the race to the end, we need to enter into rest. If we fail to do so, we will burn out quickly. If we desire a long-term ministry we must take care of our system. In Matthew 25:1–12, Jesus tells the story of the ten young bridesmaids who awaited the arrival of their bridegroom. Five were ready for his arrival at some unearthly hour because they had prepared for it, but the other five were described by Jesus as foolish because they had neglected preparation and were caught unready and unawares. These foolish bridesmaids then approached those who had brought sufficient oil to keep their own lamps burning brightly in the event of any delay, and asked if they would let them have some of their oil. 'But the wise answered, saying, "Not so; lest there be not enough for us and you: but go ye rather to them that sell, and buy for yourselves"' (Mt. 25:9, KJV). Jesus makes the telling comment that the wise said no! Wise leaders still need to know when to say no. If the wise bridesmaids had given up their own precious oil to the foolish, then there would have been insufficient for them all. Many Christian workers have discovered to their cost the truth of that scenario. Failing to learn when to say no to the apparently righteous demands being made upon us is a vital step towards wholeness for Christian workers. Taking regular and protected periods of rest replenishes our oil supply.
- *Healthier living.* It does not take an expert in pain research to work out that muscle spasm is a big

factor in most pain. Tight muscles produce pain, and no matter how relaxed you may feel, if you have chronic pain, your muscles are in spasm somewhere. Whenever pain occurs, muscle spasm is involved, often as a reflex reaction. If we touch a hot plate with our hands, the muscles of the arm react without us thinking about it. They jerk the hand away from the danger by means of an instantaneous muscle spasm for which we should be constantly grateful. Victims of the dreadful disease leprosy do not have that reaction, because their ability to feel pain has been destroyed by their underlying medical condition. As a result, when they burn their hands, fingers and toes, they are unaware of the event. Their muscles do not react in the usual lifesaving way. In the end, fingers fall off as bones contract through constant infection, the result of burns and injuries. In internal pain, muscles go into spasm to protect the site of the damage. With appendicitis, for instance, the muscles of the stomach go as hard as a board. This produces for medical students one of the classic signs used in the diagnosis of the illness. These muscle spasms are useful, protective measures taken by the body. Similarly many of the conditions associated with stress amongst Christian workers and leaders are really symptoms of failure to take adequate rest. Stomach ulcers, digestive problems, heart conditions, migraine headaches, ME and lots of other disorders may in some cases be avoided if we would learn the lessons of Sabbath.

- *Better family life*. Family life needs quality time, and Sabbath is designed to deliver it. Holidays are times of just being together and sharing each others lives. Of course, they can also be intense and difficult times when we have to face up to the tensions in our relationships and even in ourselves. For these reasons, driven people often find ways of justifying doing without holidays, pretending to be just too busy to be able to fit them in. Some of the most damaged and driven people I know have never really taken family holidays, or even meaningful time off from their responsibilities. The gift of Sabbath was given to God's people as a regular reminder that we all need space to relax and recharge, never more so than when life has put us together in families. And of course, being single does not mean you don't need to take a holiday. Spend time with friends and extended family members if you can.

- *Breaking the vicious cycle.* Rest has the ability to break cycles of pain and depression. It relaxes the grip of adrenalin overload on our system. In the case of chronic pain, for instance, the discomfort of tense muscles just adds to the pain, and also to the potential for depression. There is, therefore, a kind of cycle involved. A cycle of exhaustion and depression. Pain leads to tension which in turn leads to more pain, and so on. Within this cycle, the fear of pain also becomes a factor. Muscle tension produces pain which leads to the fear of more pain, bad posture, lack of sleep, more muscle tension and so it goes on. Sleep patterns, in particular, can suffer from the problem of disruption caused by lack of regular relaxation. I have always found sleep a very delicate creature. It is easily disturbed and flutters away. As a result I have often felt exhausted, with an almost overwhelming desire to sleep during the day. The disturbance of my sleep, as I now realise, is caused by tension in my body. An exhausted, painful body is fertile ground in which pain grows, as also do negative and fearful thoughts. All this is part of the cycle of pain and muscle spasm. The aim of relaxation is to release those muscles from their tension. The fruit of reasonably small amounts of time given over to conscious acts of relaxation on a regular basis can be manifold.

How to enter in to the Sabbath

Sabbath needs to be practised on a regular – and by that I mean daily, weekly and monthly – basis. It is the result of a change in mindset. I have mentioned before the Protestant work ethic. What about the Protestant *rest* ethic? What about the biblical basis of relaxation? God rested in his creative work. Jesus rested and relaxed even in the busiest of redemptive schedules (Mt. 14:13). Paul and his apostolic teams spent long periods walking together on their journeys, and there were long periods of rest built into the truncated record we have of the apostle's exploits in the book of Acts.

More than anyone in the Christian family, pastors and church workers need to model a different kind of lifestyle when it comes to rest. They need to be beacons in their community of an alternative to the rat race that so many are part of. They need, above all, to make a commitment, renewed regularly, to enter into God's rest themselves.

Looking after your own vineyard

True relaxation is a learned art. It does not come easily. There are many different ways of achieving it, and each has its own merits. In telling my own story I can simply say that I have found it helpful to spend time each day consciously relaxing. I do so by listening to music on my MP3 player through a pair of earphones.

I can do this without disturbing the rest of the house, and it means that I can be in a virtual world of my own for a while. I choose to listen to tapes of quiet worship songs and hymns. I find the lyrics helpful as well as the general ambience of the music. It is also helpful to me to shut my eyes and close out all distractions. I also walk a lot, and find it beneficial to do much of my praying 'on the hoof'. This has the double benefit of exercising body and soul. I have pastor friends who regularly play squash, golf or go sailing. Such pursuits must not be engaged in just for the business of making contacts for the gospel, though this is another spin-off benefit. Relaxation is a worthy aim in itself.

Part of the art of relaxation is just having eyes to see what God has placed around us. There may or may not be much in the way of natural beauty around you but there will surely be something worthy of closer attention. Eugene Peterson's vision of what he calls 'the un-busy pastor' has this element within it.[15] He asks the pertinent question of pastors and Christian leaders, 'How can I persuade a person to live by faith and not by works if I have to juggle my schedule constantly to make everything fit?' Peterson, whose achievements are not insignificant despite his emphasis on rest and include the paraphrasing of the Bible into *The Message*, speaks later of the immense value of passivity in enabling pastors to discover the true mind of God.

> Learning the art of willed passivity begins with appreciating the large and creative part passivity plays in our lives. By far the largest part of our lives is experienced in the mode of passivity. Life is undergone. We receive. We enter into what is already there. Our genetic system, the atmosphere, the food chain, our parents, the dog – they are there in place before we exercise our will...there is a willed and attentive passivity that is something more like worship.[16]

There is a very telling verse for pastors and Christian leaders in the Song of Songs (see Song 1:6) where the king's beloved regrets the fact that though she had been made the keeper of the king's vineyards, she had not kept her own vineyard well. That is so like the story of many pastors and Christian leaders, who struggle to keep the King's vineyard clean and neglect their own. We will do our churches no favours by falling apart, or for allowing our marriages to fail. We owe it to ourselves, our communities of faith and to our God to learn to look after our own vineyard too.

3

Spiritual Care

Helping others to help themselves

I heard a speaker at a leaders' conference say, 'For the most part, the best way to serve people during trials is to prepare them beforehand! Preparing ourselves and others with a biblical perspective toward trials, a biblical worldview toward suffering, gives us "roots" when the storms of life arrive.'[17] This is a neglected task of the church with regard to people in pain, but it is one that may avoid some of the pitfalls of pastoral ministry. Better to build a fence at the top of a cliff than to park an ambulance at the bottom.

I learned this vital lesson from my journeys into the African bush. In rural areas in that part of the world there is a great spirit of 'can do' amongst people. It has to be that way, because of the physical distance from help. There is no AA or RAC to call, and virtually no emergency services in those remote parts. If anything is going to be done to improve your situation, you are most likely going to have to do it yourself. As a result of this lack of outside assistance and support, rural missions workers in the Third World tend to build up an emergency kit of their own. I kept good strong tools in the vehicle, usually under the driver's seat. (Some of my colleagues built steel lockers on their vehicles to avoid the problems of the theft of tools.) I also made sure that I had powerful torches, usually designed to run off the vehicle battery. The vehicles themselves were maintained as best we could, and were chosen to be hardy and rugged rather than trendy or attractive to the eye. The state of the tyres was a matter for constant watchfulness, and the spare wheel was treated like a close friend. Nothing was left to chance. Safety and survival in this part of the world depends upon good preparation.

Similarly, in dealing with the problems of coping with storms and trauma in life, people need to be well equipped in advance to help themselves. One of the best things a Christian leader can do for their people is to prepare them beforehand to face life's trials. You can be pretty sure that such trials will come. 1 Thessalonians 3:2–4 portrays the inevitability of this fact (many other scripture passages do so too).

> We sent Timothy...to strengthen and encourage you in your faith, so that no-one would be unsettled by these trials. You know quite well that we were destined for them. In fact, when we were with you, we kept telling you that we would be persecuted. And it turned out that way, as you well know.

Despite all the advances of medical science and modern technology, as we have seen, sufferers are often on their own in facing trials. There are significant things that other people can do for them, but, on the whole, patients will do well to be prepared to help themselves, Christians or otherwise. In a very real sense, we need to assist people in building up their own toolbox! That is not to deny the role of the church in serving them in the midst of a storm, nor of the power of prayer to deliver them. But we do not just want to help and to heal but rather to teach dependence on God. Our aim is to equip others with resources to be able to cope with the challenging circumstances of their lives. 'Give a hungry man a fish,' says the proverb, 'and you feed him for a day. Teach him how to fish and you feed him and his family for life!'

After all the long years that I have battled with severe pain, I would like to suggest some simple tools that will be needed in a sufferer's toolbox.

- *Teach them the character of God.* When we seek to bring assistance to people who are in pain or all alone, we need to teach them to hope in the character of God. For this to become a reality for them, they will need two things from us. One is some help from God's Word to know what he is like. Confidence that God is good and may be relied upon in difficult times is built upon an understanding of his essential nature. God cannot lie. He is all compassionate, loving and kind towards those who are in trouble. This can be found in passages like Psalm 103 and in some of the descriptions of God's ways such as are found in the teachings of Jesus. 'No-one has ever seen God, but God the One and Only, who is at the Father's side, has made him known' (Jn. 1:18). The other thing that people will need is to see the character of God modelled in us. When they are ill, and spend long periods of time observing fellow sufferers, carers and visitors, people become quite skilled in assessing those who minister to them. They can sense genuine love and compassion, even if their situation demands that those visiting them maintain a certain 'professional distance'. They know if you care, and they sense if it is just a duty call. When we go to homes or hospital beds of the seriously ill, we are like Christ to them – just as they are to us (see Mt. 25:36).

- *Remind them of the power of God.* Hope, for the Christian believer, means trusting in the power of God. It holds on to the fact that God can do anything he wants to do, and will move in response to the heart cries of his people. I know, and keep reminding myself, that at any moment, God can turn my situation around. If he chooses not to do so, I can still be assured that nothing touches me without his permission, and that he is actively at work in the lives of those whose confidence is in him. Those who care for long-term sufferers of pain and others facing life's storms of varying kinds, need to embark upon a crusade of building hope in them (and also in themselves). There is nothing worse than those awful words, 'There's no hope.' Surely while there's life there's hope. As believers in Christ, even if we die we are the Lord's! But a cure may yet be found. Pain may come under control. God may yet step in and heal. When I was so seriously ill in Intensive Care, the word went around the churches that knew me: 'Nothing short of a miracle will save Eric now. There is no other hope for him.' Thank God they did not stop praying at that point, but pressed through to bring my situation to the God of miracles.
- *Tell them it's not their fault.* We must avoid making the mistake of presuming that whenever a Christian is suffering, their failure to receive release is a sign that their faith is weak. On the contrary, it can take a great deal more faith to face prolonged trials and remain in a place of quiet trust in God than to receive a miracle and walk away free. Over the years that I have struggled with chronic illness, there have

been several well-meaning Christians who have tried to point out to me that I was suffering because of my inadequate faith in Christ the healer. Despite all the times I have sought prayer for healing, and the occasions on which God has continued to graciously use me to bring healing to others, these allegations stung because they resonated with my confusion and guilt. This kind of approach can be so cruel and unfair to those who are daily pledging their faith in God's Word and seeking to obey.

Margie Willers deals with this problem in her wonderful book about healing and disability. She had travelled 10,000 miles from New Zealand to Los Angeles to be present at a healing service being led by the famous author and healing evangelist Kathryn Kuhlman. At the start of the service she was approached by an usher who told her that he felt she was going to be healed that night of the cerebral palsy that had kept her in a wheelchair from childhood. The usher prayed for her all through the long hours of the service, urging her to reach out and take the healing that he believed was for her, and which was being experienced by others in the huge auditorium.

> Around me the service continued unabated, but by now I was only vaguely aware of what was happening...so intent was I on stretching my faith to receive the long awaited and promised healing.[18]

Yet nothing happened, despite all Margie's longing, and the usher who had prayed with her for all those long hours became perplexed. He seemed to imply that it was Margie's fault that she was not yet healed. He urged her not to go away disappointed but to *try* again. But all the trying in the world wasn't going to bring Margie the healing for which she longed on this occasion – God had other plans for her. She went on to become the leader of a powerful ministry to disabled people, something she could not have done without her wheelchair. Yet that usher caused her untold heartache by implying that the only reason for the absence of her healing was her lack of active faith.

- *Remind them that recovery is a team task.* At the end of the day the goal of all healing ministries whether sacred or secular, is wholeness. That is a team task. Recovery of good health is a partnership between doctor and patient. Doctors have no magic wands. They are not miracle workers. They need our cooperation, and our understanding concerning their limitations. We will greatly help ourselves if we remember that fact, but even more so if we focus our trust in God. Our families are also part of the team, especially our spouse if we are married. I am really blessed that Diane does not seem to resent the fact that I am ill, but continues to stand with me 100 per cent in owning this problem as 'our problem'. The church fellowship is also part of the therapeutic team. How sad it is that sometimes the church is more of as hindrance than a help, bringing pressure and condemnation to bear upon the sick one, instead of compassion and loving kindness. Pastors and house group leaders have a part to play. Seldom did anyone ever get well in a vacuum. Recovery is a team sport.
- *Warn them of the high cost of legalism.* It has surprised me over the years of pastoral ministry the number of times I have met people who have been scrupulously careful about keeping all the 'rules' of the Christian life but who exhibit little or no genuine faith in

God when trouble comes. This attitude will almost invariably rob people of a speedy recovery, and also of the grace required to sustain them in long-term chronic sickness or pain. Any kind of faith that is built on self-effort is destined to end in disappointment, especially when storms come. Legalism is an attempt to establish our own righteousness by acts of obedience and law-keeping, and it invariably brings us into condemnation and fear. God will allow situations to come about in our lives to challenge and deepen our trust in him, for this is the issue upon which our relationship with him is founded. I once came across a helpful checklist which enables us to see if legalism is present in our lives. It said you were likely to be legalistic if you were more aware of your sin than the cross of Jesus Christ; if you thought, believed or felt God was disappointed in you (as opposed to delighting in you); if you harboured any sense that the forgiveness and acceptance of God was dependent on your obedience; if you lacked joy; and lastly, if you felt a certain amount of guilt or even a crippling condemnation, assuming perhaps that that promoted holiness.[19]

Those Christians who can see themselves here may well be struggling with legalism and finding it hard to trust God in all circumstances. Their Christian confidence is built on their own sense of achievement – of having kept God's righteous demands as they understand them. We need to reflect again on the lessons of God's amazing grace, and recognise that our salvation is based upon the objective work of Christ on the cross on our behalf. That never changes, even when the storm is raging.

This is where a simple but firm return to God's Word and his promises can do so much to restore the balance. There can also be a significant partnership in recovery between those who suffer, those who pray, and those who gently remind the sufferer of God's goodness, love and grace to us through Christ.

Preparing ourselves and others for surviving storms is about growing in real trust in God. Trusting in God is really another way of saying relaxing in God's love for us.

Vulnerability in the pulpit

If ever people in the pew are to become more real with one another and with God, then reality must begin in the pulpit. I have made it a principle that in preaching, though I do not like to mention myself, I do not hide the fact that I have been through extremely adverse circumstances. Invariably, at the close of a service or meeting I will see one or two people hanging back while I greet others. These people appear ill at ease, and are obviously waiting for the crowd to thin. Eventually they come forward to introduce themselves. More often than not they will confide that it was such a relief to them to hear the speaker say that he had been through such circumstances. It meant a lot to them – even though I did not offer any real solutions to their pain – just to know that they were not alone in their need.

Within the post-modern Western setting, the issue of vulnerability in leaders really matters. If contemporary preachers come across as authoritarian, they will be perceived as arrogant and considered to be inauthentic. When we present our teaching to contemporary audiences we must do so with humility and vulnerability. These days the way we present the truth can be as influential as the truth itself.[20]

Whether today's discerning listeners decide in favour of a speaker's proposals or not will depend on certain perceptions of the speaker by the audience. The listeners will be evaluating their sincerity. These days perceived sincerity is very high on the agenda. If the speaker's message is consistent with their lives, that is, if it appears to work for them, that will secure them a hearing. If not, it becomes a real turn-off. People are no longer asking the question 'Is it true?' but rather 'Does it work for you?' They are looking for transparency, reality, and sincerity and know only too quickly when those qualities are absent.

There is nothing new about this. In ancient classical literature there were three factors that were felt to be involved in the process of what was called rhetoric – effective spoken communication. They were *logos* which was the verbal content of the message, *pathos* which referred to the emotional aspect of the message (the passion, fervour, and the feeling with which the speaker conveyed their ideas), then finally there was *ethos* or the perceived character or credibility of the speaker. Much as you might expect, Jesus, who was a master communicator, exhibited all three.

In the Sermon on the Mount there are many signs that Jesus identified with the crowds and understood their world. He was neither aloof nor distant, but vulnerable and available. His teaching was marked by authenticity and sincerity. This was probably one of the main reasons for the approval of his teaching expressed by the crowd in Matthew 7:28 and 29. 'When Jesus had finished saying these things, the crowds were amazed at his teaching, because he taught as one who had authority, and not as their teachers of the law.' This followed on from his teaching about the need for consistency and obedience in putting into practise the teachings he had

just brought them. Jesus was perceived by the crowd to
be the living example of what he was saying. Preaching
today needs to tend towards the personal rather than
the abstract, and will be a sharing of self rather than
simply the sharing of ideas. The era of cool professional
distance between speaker and people is over, and may
now be a liability. For people in pain it is way past its
sell-by date.

Conclusion

So, the local church needs to be a place of healing in more ways than one. When its members suffer pain, then all should suffer with them, according to 1 Corinthians 12:26. This is not always the case, and special attention needs to be given to ways of shepherding the sick, especially in Pentecostal and charismatic settings. Perhaps God is even delaying his healing touch to see how the Christian community will respond to the needy ones placed within it.

The church has responsibilities for practical care towards the needy but also towards those engaged in caring, whether within institutions such as hospitals or carers in the home. Isolation must be guarded against, whether by visitation, setting the solitary in families or using self-help groups.

The local church is also called to be involved in sufferer's emotional care, and it is here that we have so often failed in the past. Church communities should be teaching and modelling the principles of Sabbath rest and relaxation in God's love... not forgetting the importance, too, of touch. Leaders should be exercising care for their own emotional welfare in order to encourage those whom they lead to do the same. Then there is the whole area of spiritual care for the suffering, and the best way to approach this is to help people to help themselves. Preparing the members of the church to go through hard times and remain victorious is as important as being there when those times come. It is in this spiritual area once again that a speaker's vulnerability about themselves in the pulpit can really take the pressure off sufferers in the congregation, who can then identify with them so much more readily.

Epilogue

There is a kind of preparation that cannot be found in University....It is that which God sovereignly ordains for a specific purpose and which drives us to our knees and to tears.[21]

Trying to understand the reason why

I was lying in bed convalescing. Diane was busy dusting, and we were chatting about some of the problems of pastoral life.

'Wouldn't it be great,' I said, 'if there was a crash course in Christian discipleship that we could put people onto after they have joined the church – a sort of shortcut to maturity in Christ?'

'Oh I know,' Diane agreed, 'like the Alpha course,[22] only for believers.'

'That's right,' I nodded, 'because there's so much immaturity in the churches.'

We regularly conduct this kind of conversation in our home. It serves as a sort of release valve for the frustration of working with people.

'Yes, that's what we need,' I said, thoughtfully, 'then people could go on this short course, and come out as fully grown Christians!' Diane stopped dusting. 'But there *is* such a course, you know.'

I frowned.

'It's called "suffering!"' she said.

We laughed, but we both knew that she was right. We also knew that no one in their right mind would apply to go on that particular course, however good the teaching or the outcome might be.

But that is what the Bible teaches. James, the brother of Jesus, writing to the early Christians, said

> Consider it pure joy, my brothers, whenever you face trials of many kinds, because you know that the testing of your faith develops perseverance. Perseverance must finish its work so that you may be mature and complete, not lacking anything. (Jas. 1:2–4)

James' apostolic colleague Paul also felt the same way about suffering. This was despite the fact that he was a firm believer in healing and had seen many miracles himself: 'we also rejoice in our sufferings,' said the famous apostle, 'because we know that suffering produces perseverance; [*and*] perseverance [*produces*] character' (Rom. 5:3b,4a – *brackets mine*).

It is never easy to understand why bad things happen to good people. The fact that they do can shake the foundations of our faith. It is fine to believe in God when the sun is shining and everything feels good, but when the sky clouds over and the going gets tough, we are tempted to wonder if our faith was just wishful thinking. Chronic and acute pain can test one's concept of God's love to its absolute limits. I know that my heavenly Father really loves me, for instance, but there have been times of such acute and prolonged agony that I know I would not leave any pet of mine for that long without intervening, probably to have them put down. 'You wouldn't let a dog suffer like that!' is a cry that strikes at the heart of the love relationship that believers have with God, and Diane and I have said it often over the years about others and about ourselves.

Some, in an effort to excuse the Lord in these difficult circumstances, have formed the view that God created the world and then left us to get on with our own devices. Their universe is open, with a 'God' who gets up each morning and asks in a rather Microsoft-like way 'Where would you like to go today?' This subtle form of mistaken faith may be an honest attempt to explain suffering, and even to 'allow' God to come out of it with his reputation intact, but it will not do if we are to be biblically correct. I am convinced that there is a loving purpose behind everything that touches my life as a child of God. Life is not just a series of random events of which some are 'good luck' and others just 'bad luck'. God has not just set his creation going and then withdrawn to a safe distance, leaving the world to fate or other face-less forces of chance. Suffering, for the Christian, is neither without purpose nor meaning. Yet in order to believe this, it is necessary to take real steps of faith and to do so willingly. Jerry Bridges says

> The truth we must believe is that God is sovereign. He carries out His own good purposes without ever being thwarted, and He so directs and controls all events and all actions of His creatures that they never act outside of His sovereign will. We must believe this and cling to this in the face of adversity and tragedy, if we are to glorify God by trusting Him.[23]

The problem of cultural expectations

In our Western culture there is too high an expectation that life should feel good in order for it to be good. When suffering and trials come we are shocked and surprised that these things happen in a believer's life. This ignores the fact that today, in two-thirds of the world, Christians are suffering want or need, and in many cases being persecuted for their faith. This expectation of ease is also contrary to the New Testament which warns us that 'In fact, everyone who wants to live a godly life in Christ Jesus will be persecuted' (2 Tim. 3:12) and that 'We must go through many hardships to enter the kingdom of God' (Acts 14:22). In our materialistic society, however, the 'feel-good factor' is very important in every area of public and private life. It is so in our politics, for instance, but it has also crept into church thinking. It is no longer popular to preach about suffering for Christ unless it's in very far-off places. Many preachers who travel frequently in a westerly direction find their theology moulded as a result of what they witness there. They would do well to go east or south for a change! They would find a very different, but no less vibrant, kind of Christianity. In fact, the very life and faith of the church in the Third World challenges what believers in the West feel we need to have in order to feel good. God's people there may be poor in material goods, but they are rich in spirit!

My occasional preaching visits in the past to slum churches in India have shown me this fact. Packed with worshipping, loving believers, they are a joy to behold. Yet, because many of the converts come from the 'untouchable' classes of India's Hindu caste system, they continue to be among the poorest of the poor. They no longer qualify for government aid, and live in shanty dwellings on the outskirts of some of the world's largest cities. Their riches are in Christ. They rejoice in God's abundant goodness to them. Yet in terms of material goods, their hands are empty. For Christians in two-thirds of God's world, there is no expectation that the Christian life will be devoid of suffering and pain, or that the lack of these things is any kind of evidence of faith!

So the idea that life should always *feel* good in order to *be* good is not necessarily shared by people in other cultures. Some of them seem to have a higher understanding of the place of pain, and even death, in the pattern of life. In general terms there is a clearer perception of the reality of the spiritual world alongside the material. They know that what they own materially is not *all* that they own. Life, for them, can be very blessed despite the most appalling circumstances.

Television

This situation is changing, of course, with the spread of access to television. This transports the viewer out of their own culture and shows them ideas and values mostly imported from the West. Diane and I were resident as missionaries in one remote Indian Ocean island at the time when television was first introduced into that community. Although the medium was primitive in its methods, particularly in local programme productions, it did serve as a platform for imported Western viewing, mostly of a very low quality. The islanders, who up until that time were a peaceable and gentle people, were suddenly thrown into the mêlée of big-time crime and Western moral standards (or lack of them). The result was a noticeable change in the social atmosphere. Crime began to increase, and became more violent. Television began to change a society. The expectations of islanders were also changing. Into their shanty homes were coming images of unimaginable wealth and bounty. Previously fairly contented as a race, the islanders became noticeably more acquisitive, and an air of unrest began to spread as we were leaving. We·hear from friends still resident there that the situation has worsened since.

Television was not the only negative influence, but it played its part in the downturn. Nowadays, I am told, in that exquisite island paradise, whilst there is still a long way to go before the situation is anything like as bad as it is in some places, there is a new atmosphere of social unease.

In a related but different way, I really do feel that Christian TV, as it is being introduced to Europe at the moment, and as has widely been available for some time in the USA, has the same power to unsettle and confuse suffering Christians. There is an image of wealth, fame and success that accompanies the programmes, and encourages believers to expect that all their troubles will be over if they learn to exercise faith for final victory over Satan. Indeed, the dangers of some kinds of Christian television could be compared with the effects of pornography – making a Christian dissatisfied with his local church just like a man might become dissatisfied with his wife because of an artificial sexuality portrayed on the screen. They may become enchanted with the constantly available and always successful kind of Christianity that they see on television instead of recognising the blessings they already have in their church, home or marriage, even in adversity.

Compounding this false image there is the problem that television as a medium is not the best way to portray spiritual truth, focusing as it does by necessity on the outward and the physical. It is probably due to the obvious high cost of Christian television that it seems to have become a vehicle for a particular brand of so-called 'faith and prosperity' teaching. Whilst there may be tremendous potential for good in television produced by Christian ministries, there is also the potential for exactly the opposite.

Support

Christians in the developing world are also usually better equipped to handle the tragic events of life. When death comes, for instance, they are often far more adequately supported in their grief than we are in the West.

Their support is firstly internal, because their faith is uncluttered by possessions and gives them a firm grasp on the reality of heaven. The expectations that they have of this life are cut more according to the pattern of the realities of their situation – and their vulnerability. Secondly, they have much stronger support usually from within their family structure and the attitude of the community, Christian and otherwise, to the issue of death and grief. The whole process of grieving over such loss is often a drawn-out one, with the free expression of feelings and great ritual. But sufferers are never left alone; not when they are ill, nor when they are grieving over the loss of loved ones.

People in those kinds of situations may have little in this life, but they do have each other. This resource is shared widely and freely, often to the great frustration of employers from other cultures when they see their workforce decimated by those attending weddings and funerals!

In our culture, though, we expect certain rights and even demand them. Our presumption is that if we trust God and especially if we serve God, major troubles and trials will not visit our home. When it comes to biblical expectations, however, Christians are warned only to expect a cross. In the line up of rights, our primary right is an execution gibbet. In this regard I can't help thinking of the words of Jesus to his first group of full-time workers.

If anyone would come after me, he must deny himself and take up his cross daily and follow me. (Lk. 9:23)

During all my illness, I have from time to time overheard someone say that I did not deserve to be so unwell. I understand their motives in doing so. They reckoned that as a full-time Christian worker it somehow ought not to be. I agreed with them at first. But my considered response now is to be grateful that I have never received what I *do* deserve in this life! That is not to indulge in any kind of false humility, but rather to be realistic. After all, as one who previously rejected Christ, and ignored what he did for me on the cross to my own peril, the only thing I deserved was God's wrath and judgement. It is by God's grace that we can expect anything at all in a fallen world – but thankfully, in Christ, that grace is freely given. The fact that we are loved by God at all is so amazing. Yet he who knows us totally loves us completely and unconditionally.

A view from eternity

The good things of God are always viewed from eternity. That's his vantage point. He is above the horizon of time and higher than the clouds of our pain. I love flying, and one of the joys for me of being a missionary was the opportunity to do quite a lot of it. There is nothing quite like the exhilaration of boarding an aircraft on an overcast day, taking off, and then a few minutes later breaking through the cloud cover into glorious sunshine above. It's amazing that when things are so dark down below, the glory of the sun can be blazing above. God's 'good' is the good that sees things from above the clouds. Jerry Bridges again

The good that God works for in our lives is conformity to the likeness of His Son. It is not necessarily comfort or happiness but conformity to Christ in ever-increasing measure in this life and in its fullness in eternity.[24]

This is surely at the root of Paul's comment in Romans 8:28. The phrase 'called according to his purpose' makes it plain. The 'all things' depend upon us loving God and his purposes for our lives. Outside those parameters, there is no blanket assurance for Christians just because of our faith. But within the purposes of God, and our love of him and them, there is a sense of peace. He will work it out for good.

There have been many occasions when my wife and I have shrugged and said, 'I expect that comes into the category of the "all things".' We don't understand it now, and perhaps don't need to. God's perspective is different to ours. 'As the heavens are higher than the earth, so are my ways higher than your ways and my thoughts than your thoughts' (Is. 55:9). It was this higher perspective that enabled New Testament believers to go through appalling trials and yet keep the faith. When Paul encountered that storm on his way to Rome – clearly the specific will of God for his life – he simply could not have known that the storm would throw them up on the beach in Malta where it appears that God had an appointment for Paul with the island's chief official.

This concept of God's higher good has kept me sane during the years I was ill in the 1990s and the long period more recently when I have been ill again... *years* of battling with pain. Despite being utterly frustrated at times at not being able to preach, or to function in any kind of ministry other than that which I could do from a place of weakness, I know that God was doing something in me. I will not be the same again. Paul's storm took him to a place where he would never have gone of his own free will. My storm has blown me right off my own course, but I know that God will have his own way, and the end result will be good.

I remember hearing Pastor Paul (now David) Yonggi Cho preach. He is the Senior Pastor of the world's largest church, Full Gospel Church in Seoul, Korea. He was telling of the days of persecution that the believers have known in Korea. He talked about pastors buried up to their necks in sand and left to die in the sun. He portrayed graphically the suffering of Christians whose families and homes were taken from them. Certainly in Korea, the blood of the martyrs has been the seed of the church! Alongside the massive Full Gospel Church, some other denominations have their largest congregation in the world in Korea. It is said that the Christian church in that land is growing faster than the birth-rate. Korea is on its way to becoming a Christian nation. Yet, at what cost? Pastor Cho based his talk on the idea, taken from the book of Psalms, of God sitting as King for ever, and ruling over the floods (see Ps. 29:10, KJV). I shall never forget the sense of the majesty and the overruling power of God that I felt that day. Suffering and loss is not the end of the story when King Jesus rules over our lives.

Pain changes perspective

I have learned all the lessons in this book the hard way. Yet, I am sometimes not sure if I have learnt them at all. Pain has an urgency about it that is all-consuming. When pain strikes and takes hold of us, it threatens to throttle out our theology completely. Even our faith comes under fire. This is, of course, the reason why interrogators resort to torture in their efforts to get prisoners of war to talk. No matter how high their ideals, or noble their intentions, pain has the power to break their resolve. As I said before – and I state it again because I think it is important – I understand that one of the most effective ways to withstand torture is to 'reckon that you are dead already'. Apparently – and I remember reading this in the account of a torture victim who had survived dreadful assaults on himself – to imagine that you are dead already equips you with an unbreakable resignation. This attitude among prisoners is respected by even some of the most hardened of interrogators. They know that they can do no more to frighten the individual who reckons himself dead already.

This concept is not new. The writers of the New Testament were aware of this secret of survival. 'In the same way, count yourselves dead to sin but alive to God in Christ Jesus' (Rom. 6:11). This speaks metaphorically about the war that rages between the spirit and the flesh in the life of a believer. It also holds true, though, in terms of the adversities we face. Pain, and in particular, acute pain, does sometimes demand that we resign ourselves to just going through it. An attitude of quiet resignation and acceptance enabled me to bear the most horrendous indignities and assaults upon my body during my prolonged stay in Intensive Care. I reckoned that I was dead to my feelings anyway, but alive to God. I found it helpful to just turn my mind away from the throbbing realities of the flesh, and to try to visualise the Lord. It may sound pretentious to say this, but I found great comfort in 'seeing' the Lord Jesus in his sufferings on the cross. On the occasion when my epidural anaesthesia failed and I was in unspeakable pain, I remembered that

the Lord had refused the anaesthetic of those days –
wine and gall vinegar – in order to identify fully with
human suffering, and I was comforted. I knew that he
suffered the most terrible death, and overcame it. From
his endurance, and subsequent victory, I derived hope.
Maybe in some small way I was learning one special
meaning of the phrase, 'the fellowship of sharing in his
sufferings' (Phil. 3:10).

Pain does change our perspective, but not God's. He
is still in charge. I am not embarrassed by this statement
of faith. It is true. Pain would attempt a cover-up of
that fact, but faith lays hold of it even in the dark.

God *is* in charge.

Just to help you...

Ten fear-fighting Bible texts

Isaiah 41:10
So do not fear, for I am with you; do not be dismayed, for I am your God. I will strengthen you and help you; I will uphold you with my righteous right hand.

Deuteronomy 20:3b,4
Do not be faint-hearted or afraid; do not be terrified or give way to panic before [*your enemies*], for the LORD your God is the one who goes with you to fight for you against your enemies to give you victory.

1 Chronicles 28:20
...Be strong and courageous, and do the work. Do not be afraid or discouraged, for the LORD God, my God, is with you. He will not fail you or forsake you...

Isaiah 43:1,2
But now, this is what the LORD says – he who created you, O Jacob, he who formed you, O Israel: 'Fear not, for I have redeemed you; I have summoned you by name; you are mine. When you pass through the waters, I will be with you; and when you pass through

the rivers, they will not sweep over you. When you walk through the fire, you will not be burned; the flames will not set you ablaze.'

Psalm 27:1
The LORD is my light and my salvation – whom shall I fear? The LORD is the stronghold of my life – of whom shall I be afraid?

Psalm 118:6
The LORD is with me; I will not be afraid. What can man do to me?

Proverbs 29:25
Fear of man will prove to be a snare, but whoever trusts in the LORD is kept safe.

Hebrews 13:5,6
...because God has said, 'Never will I leave you; never will I forsake you.' So we say with confidence, 'The Lord is my helper; I will not be afraid. What can man do to me?'

2 Timothy 1:7
For God did not give us a spirit of timidity, but a spirit of power, of love and of self-discipline.

Psalm 56:3,4.
When I am afraid, I will trust in you. In God, whose word I praise, in God I trust; I will not be afraid. What can mortal man do to me?

A prayer for times of pain

Lord, you know how I feel today without me spelling it out, but I want to tell you again about my pain. [*Just describe simply and honestly what is happening to you*] I praise you that you are in charge of my life, and that with you, nothing is wasted. I ask for strength and grace to go on another day. I pray for the ability to forgive those who have hurt me. Lord, grant me the ability to rest and even relax in your love today, knowing that you are my healer and the One who keeps me going till my healing comes to its fullness. Into your hands, Lord, I commit myself today.

Contact details:

If you have been affected by any of the issues raised in this book, and would like to contact me via Authentic Media, I would be pleased to hear from you. I would be especially happy to offer any assistance to pastors and Christian leaders or churches who would like to implement change in their care for the suffering.

    You may also contact me at:

ericgaudion@hotmail.com

Endnotes

1. From the song 'Blessed Be Your Name' by Matt & Beth Redman. Copyright © 2002 Thankyou Music. Adm. By worshiptogether.com songs excl. UK & Europe, adm. By kingswaysongs.com tym@kingsway.co.uk. Used by permission.

2. Margaret A. Caudill, MD, PhD, *Understanding Pain* (New York: The Guilford Press) 18.

3. Chris Wells and Graham Nown, *In Pain* (London: Optima, 1993) introduction.

4. John Piper, *Future Grace* (Grand Rapids, MI: Baker House Books, 1995) 9.

5. Rick Warren, *The Purpose Driven Life* (Grand Rapids, MI: Zondervan, 2002). See also www.purposedrivenlife.com

6. Helen Roseveare, *Digging Ditches*, (Tain, Rossshire: Christian Focus Publications, 2005) 81.

7. Brother Yun with Paul Hattaway, *The Heavenly Man* (London: Monarch Books, 2002).

8. See www.aglimpseofeternity.org

9. I would strongly recommend reading Dr R.T. Kendall's book, *Total Forgiveness: achieving God's greatest challenge* (London: Hodder & Stoughton, 2001).

10. Margery Williams, *The Original Velveteen Rabbit* or *How Toys Become Real* (London: Egmont Books, 1922).

11. Fentanyl is a narcotic analgesic used primarily for analgesia during surgery and to supplement other

anaesthetics. It is also used on skin patches to control extreme pain. One of its very rare side-effects is that it can occasionally suppress breathing.

12. Quoted in Paul Brand and Philip Yancey, *Pain – The Gift Nobody Wants* (London: Marshall Pickering, 1997).

13. Jerry Bridges, *Trusting God, Even When Life Hurts* (Amersham: Scripture Press, 1996) 48.

14. Paul Brand and Philip Yancey, *Pain – The Gift Nobody Wants* (London: Marshall Pickering, 1997) 275.

15. Eugene Peterson, *The Contemplative Pastor: Returning to the Art of Spiritual Direction* (Grand Rapids, MI: Eerdmans, 1993) 17.

16. Ibid., 106,107.

17. Joe McMullin is a leader with Sovereign Grace Ministries in the USA, and made this statement at a Small Group Leaders' Conference in Washington, November 1997.

18. Margie Willers, *Awaiting the Healer* (Eastbourne: Kingsway, 1991) 81.

19. See C.J. Mahaney, Article 'Surveying the Wondrous Cross' in *Sovereign Grace Magazine*, Jan/Feb 1998.

20. See Robertson McQuilkin, 'Connecting with Postmoderns' in 'Leadership' archives at www.christianitytoday.com/leaders

21. Dr R.T. Kendall, *God Meant It For Good* (Eastbourne: Kingsway, 1995), rear cover.

22. *Alpha* is the name given to a course of evangelistic messages, given either by a speaker, or on a video, following a meal. The course was pioneered by the Holy Trinity Church, Brompton, London, and is enormously successful. It is now being used by churches of all denominations across many nations.

23. Bridges, *Trusting God*, 52.

24. Ibid., 120.